CHASING THE RAINBOW

Facilitating a Pagan Festival Without Losing Your Mind

Tish Owen

Copyright © 2007 by Tish Owen

All rights reserved.

This book may not be reproduced in whole or in part, by microfilm or xerography, or any other means, mechanical or electronic, without permission, except as noted.

Previously published by Willow Tree Press

ISBN-13: 978-0-9996327-8-9

Cover Design Copyright © 2007 Johnathan Minton

Cover Photo Copyright ©2007 On The Edge Photography

Interior Book Design by K. J. Epps

Interior Photos courtesy of PUF attendees, staff and On The Edge Photography

10 9 8 7 6 5 4 3 2 1

PRINTED IN THE U.S.A.

To my father, Robert Edward Hickman,
who taught me that there are more things
in heaven and on earth than I had dreamt of…
I continue to find them.

CONTENTS

Author's Note – *Why?*	ix
Acknowledgements	xiii
Introduction - *Not enough medication*	1
What Kind of Festival? - *You mean I get to pick?*	4
Getting Help - *Ask and ye shall receive.*	13
Staff - *Who you gonna call?*	18
Organization - *How anal-retentive are you?*	25
Festival Site - *Do not try this at home!*	29
Advertising - *If you build it, they won't come, unless they know about it.*	33
Pre-Registration - *Don't guess who's coming to dinner.*	37
The Kid Thing - *It takes a village and then some.*	41
Workshops/Classes - *Here be dragons.*	49
Merchants - *Cool things to buy!*	55
Maps - *Directions! What a concept!*	58
Ritual - *Seating for 200, please.*	60
Problems and Complaints - *Murder is illegal.*	66
Things You Need To Bring - *Hammers, saws and drain cleaner*	74
Things They Need To Bring - *Don't leave home without it.*	78
How To Buy Food - *Measure twice, cut once.*	82
Recipes - *Yum! Yum!*	92
Friends, Neighbors and the Media - *Oh, my!*	104
Big Party - *The drums, the drums, the drums!*	107
Program - *Opportunity for cute cartoons*	110
Big-Nose Pagans - *Warts and all*	123
Police Politics - *How to handle the authorities*	128
Volunteers - *You want me to do what?*	134
Forms - *KISS*	137
Rules - *We don't need no stinkin' rules!*	144
PUF Stories - *Once upon a time…*	148
Guests - *Pack a bag. We are going to the festival!*	164
Last But Not Least - *Twenty-five rules for a festival organizer*	168
Index	173

Author's Note
Why?

This is dedicated to all you tireless, sleep deprived, caffeine-cranked, bug bitten, sunburned, insane people who run festivals for the Pagan folk in this world. You have a tremendous amount of intestinal fortitude, an amazing work ethic and a genuine caring for the community at large. Plus, you are nuts and should probably be in a home somewhere for most of the year.

For those of you who have never done it, please know that running a festival is not about making a lot of money. Most don't. Most organizers are very happy to break even and consider an event to be successful if there are only a few dollars left over at the end of the weekend. Hell, some of us consider an event to be successful if it only loses a little bit of money. Our first festival went into the hole by $4.00. Before you complain about how much money a festival admission costs, consider what went into that festival. Even toilet paper is not cheap these days.

Running a festival is not about being the Big-Nose Witch. If that is your motivation, put the book down and go be a rock star. It is hard to feel self-important when you are unstopping a toilet at 3 A.M. To further take the wind out of your sails, add into the mix the number of people who come to you constantly over the course of the festival to bitch at you. They will happily tell you about all your shortcomings and all of the things you did wrong and all of the things that you do not do. They will even look you up after the festival and dump on you a little more. Not good for the old ego. But it does service to keep the head-swelling at a minimum.

Running a festival is not about looking good and floating around the site in a shimmering, gossamer ritual garb outfit, looking like something off an episode of *Charmed*. Usually you are wearing cut-offs, a tee shirt and a silly hat. Or is that only me? Anyway, usually you look like hammered dammit because you have not had sleep in three days and your nose is peeling from the sunburn. (Where did you pack that sunscreen?) You are lucky if you remember or have time to brush your teeth each morning of festival. Yeah, you are looking good, baby.

Unless you have ever organized a festival, you don't understand all the shifting, changing, adjustments and hourly nervous breakdowns that go into it. You have no idea of the countless hours of work, worry, shopping, cooking, organizing, sweating over money and people herding that it entails. What makes it even harder is that the people you are herding are Pagans. That is a lot like herding cats or trying to nail Jell-O to a tree. It takes real dedication and perseverance and sometimes a psychotic break with reality to achieve.

If you love going to festivals, the next time before you leave site, pick up some trash, help load a van and take a moment to thank the folks who worked so hard to provide the weekend for you. Believe me that every "Thank-you" that a festival organizer gets fills us with joy and satisfaction. Every "What a great time we had" makes us remember why we do what we do. And every "I can't wait till next year" brings tears to our eyes. I am not kidding, nor am I being sappy…okay, maybe a little sappy. It is hard work, and most folks who run festivals do not sleep the week before or during the festival and spend countless hours putting out fires, real ones and otherwise. When we lay down at night (or usually in the wee hours of the morning), we are so wired we can't sleep. Sometimes when we are in the thick of it, we don't realize how well it is going and how much fun is being had. So, pat your local festival organizer on the head; they deserve it. They are probably the hardest working folks you will ever meet. Pardon the shameless self-promotion, but festival organizers need love too.

In light of all that, why the hell do we do it? For the community. No really, quit laughing, I mean it. That really is why. So that the Pagan community will have someplace that is safe and neutral where they may come together. So that Pagans will get the opportunity to see Pagan authors in their local area and not have to drive several hundred miles or pay a fortune to do so. So that solitaries and newbies will have a place to learn some hands-on stuff and not just have to learn from books. So that 100 or 200 or 500 Pagans of different trads and paths and clans and covens and groves can come together and stand inside sacred space and blend their energies with each other and the powers that be. So that those same Pagans can come to know each other, to exchange ideas and have conversations with folks that walk a very different path, and each person can develop an understanding of the other. So that we can learn to work together. So that we can learn to love one another. So that we can understand that we must support one another. So that we can know that in times of trial we will lift up one another. So that we can finally understand that, no matter what our differences are, our samenesses are what really matter. (Wow, I have broken out in a sweat! Can I get a hallelujah?)

Add into the tally for doing this madness this little fact: for every person who bitches about something (and the list is endless and sometimes insane), there are fifty that praise all the hard work. Pagans are not shy about it either; they come to you and tell you what a good time they had, they slap you on the back and brag on you. That makes it worth all the work. Damn, we work hard for praise!

Besides all of that, it is fun! It is one big, crazy party, and you get to see friends that you only see once in a while or maybe only once a year. You get to catch up and find out what is happening in their world and vice versa. Everyone lets his or her hair down a little (or a lot) and everyone has a good time. You eat too much, drink too much, laugh too much and hang out with like-minded folks, and you're usually in the woods. What could be better?

Why did I write this little book? Because it seems that there are more and more people out there attempting to create Pagan festivals from scratch. They have no guidance, only a good idea. They have no list of "dos and don'ts" to go by, only perseverance. They don't really know where to start, and so sometimes the starting can be very rocky. I hear a lot of complaints that there are too many people trying to do festivals that have no idea what they are doing. I have heard not just bad stories but true horror stories about the lack of organization, no attention to detail, not plotting out the end results of having a couple of hundred people on a site for two or three days, not enough food, not enough space, horrible accommodations not fit for humans; the list goes on and on. The people that complain will not go back to the festivals they complain about. And those festivals will die aborning. I think that is a shame.

There are too many folks that get the great idea to have a Pagan festival and have no rock solid research on how to actually do it. They are working on the "If we build it they will come" theory. That is all fine and good to a point. It is where we started after all, but it takes more than that. I hope to provide those steps in this book.

We had a few missteps in the beginning (a few—who am I kidding?), and we just kept on reinventing the wheel. If I can save someone some of the pain and stupid mistakes that we went through, then I have done a good thing. If I can help an organizer to get their act together so that the folks who attend the festival do not suffer but actually have a great time, then everyone is happier for that.

I intend this to be a guide for Pagan festivals, Pagan Pride days, and beyond that, for anyone who wants to try their hand at some sort of a festival where you entertain, educate and feed folks, Pagan or non-Pagan. I think that the ideas and information I have included can work across the board.

If, after you read this little book, you decide to join the ranks of festival organizers, best of luck to you. You're gonna need it! You will be joining a rather elite group of folks and a brotherhood/sisterhood of shared mirth, hysteria, fun, insanity and great personal satisfaction. Welcome—and try to have some fun with it. 'Cause that, baby, is what it's all about.

☙Acknowledgements❧

There are so many people to thank for the help they have given me on the Pagan Unity Festival and in putting this book together, I fear that I may leave someone out. My husband, Patrick, who has gone down this winding road with me from the beginning, even when he knew I was nuts. My children, Michelle, who made me look great; Tanya, who praised and encouraged me; and Elf, who offered me unconditional support. The Witches of the Woods who have stepped up to the plate and worked like Nubian slaves for this endeavor; it would never have happened without them. A special thanks to Lori (without her we would all be sleeping in our cars), Beth who told me I could not use the phrase "goat screw" in this book, Billy cause I love him and he keeps me sane (mostly), Doug and Rachel who have worn many hats, Lydia, Josh and Thomas who try to entertain the teens, Mehgan and Lisa who have run my shop while I played in the woods, Lynn who herds the kids, John who keeps us secure, Jim and Dave who have taken such good care of our VIPs and Todd, Ron, Chris, Amy, Tracy, Thayer, Dawn, Rodney, Elizabeth, Shawn, Scott, Carol, Anne, Mike, Perry, Evan and everyone else who has hauled and fetched and worked like dogs. You have been my partners in crime! Oak, Ash and Thorn, Tangled Moon and S.P.I.R.A.L. Their contributions have been invaluable. All the many individuals who have pitched in, you all know who you are, and I thank you for your countless hours of work and devotion. To Debbie Fertitta and Anne Donnelly, two of my oldest friends, who held my had and made me look good for the picture. To Sydney for just being. To Barry, thanks for all the Haiku. Thanks, Mom.

PUF would not be the same without our merchants, and we have had some wonderful folks over the years. You have brought us fabulous and exotic items to tempt us, and we have succumbed to your charms. All the folks that put themselves on the line to teach workshops, bless you all. You have brought knowledge, enlightenment and fun to so many. Everyone who has taken part, written, directed and starred in the rituals. They have been great and interesting and different. I have loved every one. Our musicians, who are so wonderful. Our music has grown over the years, from none, to drummers and one guitar and finally to musical groups, so thanks to Love Drums, Labyrinthe, Celeste Alane, Laura Powers, Skinny White Chick, The Blues Bards and Jack Montgomery and his group.

Last but not least, our VIPs have made the festival great, thanks so much for taking a chance on a small and unknown festival and putting us on your schedules. We have enjoyed you all, and I feel that I have become friends with each of you. As near as I can make it here is the list; Isaac Bonewits because he is a god, M. R. Sellars because he is so damn cute, Dorothy Morrison who is the coolest, Tony Kail who is so smart, Swain Wodening who is a delight, Ashleen O'Gaia and her husband CanyonDancer who fit in so well, Grey Cat our local celeb, Trish Telesco, and Anne Moura our wonderful new friend. Thank you, thank you. Bless you for the work you do for all of us in this crazy community.

Thanks to everyone who has encouraged me to write this book, as well as the folks who have read it, corrected my English, shoved me in a different direction—a better direction—and patted me on my head. Thanks to Murv and Isaac for suggesting that I write it. Know that mere words cannot convey all that is in my heart to you. I wish you all peace, love and joy. I also have to acknowledge the most important ingredient for the success of PUF, the folks who attend. Thank you for making us a success.

Murv, you are a huge reason for our success; you have hooked us up with so many great guests and been a good friend as well. Thank you so very much.

My editor, Kat, thank you; you make me sound so smart.

If I have left anyone out, it was not by intent but by virtue of the fact that the old brain cells are not what they once were.

⋄Introduction⋄
Not enough medication

So, I run a successful Pagan festival, and this is my story. (Jeez, I sound like Sgt. Joe Friday from *Dragnet*, the old one with...well...ok...hmmm...dating myself...never mind.) Anyway, for years I read about Pagan festivals in other parts of the country, and they sounded so wonderful. I could visualize it all in my head; a gathering where Pagans would come together in harmony, sit out on blankets in the sunshine and commune with nature, where little children would run and play in the fields on a lovely spring day, where there were rituals, and people of diverse backgrounds would join one another to worship in perfect love and perfect trust. (Cue violins.)

It was a BIG picture; you know what I mean, where the entire scene fills the movie screen in your head, and you can feel the wind in your hair, the sun on your skin and smell the flowers blooming and the sunscreen on your face, all as you run through the meadow laughing. But as I ran across the fragrant fields with a silly grin on my face, I tripped over a great big rock every time. I live in the Bible Belt. The idea of a bunch of Pagans cavorting in public was a bit daunting; actually it was a little more than a bit. I could practically hear the angry mob coming over the hill with pitchforks and torches. That thought usually jolted me out of my daydream. At that point, the pretty pictures in my head would fade and become tattered and blow away like dandelion down on the breeze. After all, people in my part of the world still lose housing, jobs, friends and children because of faith issues.

Even here in the back of beyond, there were a few groups that did gatherings, but they were small and not well publicized. My own group occasionally did public rituals, usually in a park with a limited guest list. To keep from alarming the locals, we did not wave athames in the air or run about in great, black flapping cloaks. But on the occasions we met, we had such a good time, and the fellowship was great. The folks that attended always left on such a lovely spiritual high, and I grinned like a loon all the way home. Once or twice we got together with another coven and had a blast. It worked! It proved to me that Pagans from different traditions could work and play well together. This kind of success made me want to do a gathering on a larger basis. I tried to talk myself out of this crazy idea and listed for myself, over and over, all the reasons why it was a bad idea:

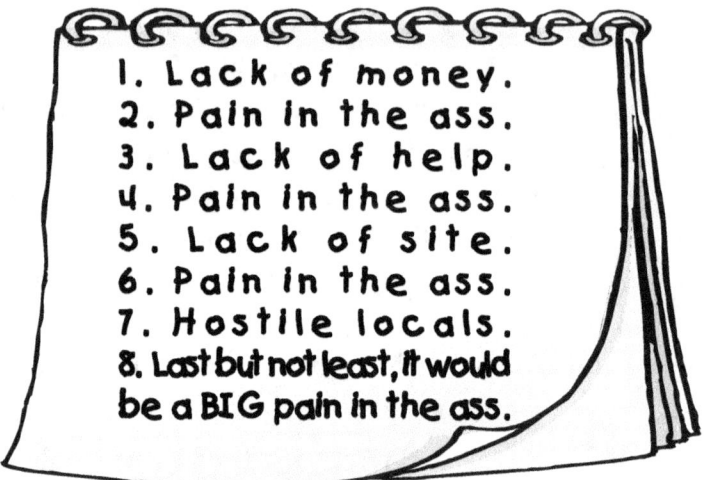

1. Lack of money.
2. Pain in the ass.
3. Lack of help.
4. Pain in the ass.
5. Lack of site.
6. Pain in the ass.
7. Hostile locals.
8. Last but not least, it would be a BIG pain in the ass.

But try as I might to exorcise it, I could not get that damn daydream to quit running in my head. It just became stronger, and the violins became louder. I was enthralled by a vision.

Every now and then the gods would smack me in the head and make me wonder if I was insane to want to do a big festival. There were several local incidents that involved angry neighbors, police officers with guns, bad press and run-ins with the local Religious Right. Some of the incidents were just stupid enough to piss me off; but some of them were down right scary, and people were placed in the path of danger. Still I thought that if I was cautious, I could manage to make it happen without too many repercussions. Hope springs eternal in the human heart, or in those of us who need more medication.

I finally started talking to the other members of my group, Witches of the Woods, about this crazy idea. After very little discussion, we decided to go for it because they are all crazy too. So in 1997 we decided to try our hands at a small festival. Believe me when I say we had no clue how to do it. Back in those days, before the rocks got hard, there were not a lot of festivals in this part of the world, or anywhere else for that matter. There was no one to ask, "How do you pull this off?" No one had written a book to tell us how to do it, and so there was no one to tell us it was an impossible task to pull off for those with very little knowledge. Like us. So, since no one had taught us how to make the wheel, we had to build it from scratch. We forged ahead…or maybe I should say we stumbled ahead. We drew on what we knew, what we had seen and most of all what we had read. If you are old enough to remember the old Mickey Rooney and Judy Garland movies, it was kind of like that. "My uncle has a barn, so let's put on a show." If you aren't that old, please don't tell me, it will only depress me.

⚘What Kind of Festival?⚘
You mean I get to pick?

Once you have decided to have a festival, you must decide what kind of festival you want to have. No, that is not how we did it, but do as I say not as I did. We have been very lucky with Pagan Unity Festival. We did not have a plan; we did not know we needed one. What we did have was a lot of folks that would be attending who had small children. Since it is illegal in this state to simply duct tape kids to trees, we had to have some activities for them. So we decided to be kid-friendly. The first year, we set up a separate site for kids within the festival and created activities for them. We felt that kids who are being raised in the Pagan path should be able to come to a festival and feel welcome. There needed to be entertaining things for them to do. That was a philosophy, not a plan.

But because it was our philosophy, our festival started out being "kid-friendly." Over the years our festival has developed the reputation for being a family event. Our reputation brings us people who want to have a good time; learn; commune with others, the gods and nature; and bring the kids along. Our reputation has kept out the folks that want to be naked, and drunk and stoned. Okay, let me amend this a bit, or it sounds like we run a church camp. There is some naked, but it is confined to cabins and tents so that the rest of us don't have to see it (although admittedly, some of us have certainly heard it). There is drinking (we have a don't ask don't tell policy with the rangers), but no one gets out of hand or acts any more stupid than usual. It is really rather amazing. If there are drugs, I have never seen any. Which is good 'cause I would hate to have to hurt someone. I really am dead set against them and believe that a Pagan festival is no place for them. Why? Illegal! Illegal! Illegal!! We are looked at askance by the general public; we cannot afford to participate in anything that is illegal. I do know that a fella came to the festival one year with a friend and combed the site looking to score a little pot; he came up empty. That makes me smile a little secret smile. I also know that a fella offered some pot to a young woman who, unbeknownst to him, was a member of the staff. She ripped his face off, and we have not seen him since. (She swears that she did not throw him in the lake with the snapping turtles, and I believe her.)

We have, over the years, created a list of rules that helps us to maintain the kind of atmosphere we have created. We spell out what kind of behavior we expect from our festival folk. Still, we know that there are people who will not come to PUF and go off and bad mouth us because of our rules. I hate that; hell, no one wants to be the subject of ugly talk. But there are plenty of festivals where folks can go to get what they are looking for, so we stick to our guns.

So, the first question you must ask yourself is: What kind of festival do you want to have? Is this to be a festival for all the Pagans in your area? Is it a festival for a certain designated group? Will it be child-friendly? Will it be for spiritual growth? Do you want to educate? Will it be an opportunity to meet others? Do you just want drunken craziness and debauchery? That is for you to decide. And decide you had better because as your festival starts out, so it grows. Unless you are just plain lucky like we have been. This is pretty weighty stuff; you are deciding the fate of your festival before you have even started.

So, let's make this easy. What kind of a festival do you like to attend? Why do you go? Is it to catch up with old friends? Do you go to make new friends? Do you go for the workshops? Do you go to see the Big-Nose Pagans? Is it a chance to go nuts and party all weekend? How about because it is fun to attend big rituals. Or is it so that you can sample different traditions? Maybe it is because you want to hang out in the woods and commune with nature. Do you go to strengthen your connection to Deity? Make a list of why you go. Next make a list of what you would like to see that you think is missing from the festivals you have attended. Did you know there would be homework with this book?

If what you want is a festival that is open and welcoming to all the paths of Paganism and that offers something for everyone, then you have a tall order. Not impossible, it just takes planning. There are many festivals that go this route; they take the "we are all in this together" view. So if this is your idea, you want to organize your festival around the groups of people whom you know will attend and offer something for everyone. You must have workshops and activities in your schedule that have a wide appeal. That means workshops for the newbies and for as many different traditions as you can entice to your festival and different kinds of rituals too. I have heard this referred to as a "General Pagan Festival."

This kind of festival is a good idea and one that we use for PUF. We encourage people from different paths and trads to come together. The festival is planned around all people on the Pagan Path. We try to have guests and workshop facilitators that have a wide range of information to disseminate. We encourage everyone to attend all the classes they can manage to get to and all the activities that interest them. We also encourage them to attend all of the rituals, no matter their chosen path. At this kind of a festival with folks from all trads and some from none, you need to encourage them to attend workshops and rituals; you have to push them to participate. This is because some Pagans are shy—yes really. It is also because they may have only studied one path and are unsure about dabbling in others. This will take work on your part.

We try to make sure that there are lots of things for folks to sample and to ensure that no one will be left out, if possible. Now, you don't have to go crazy and find the only practitioner of East-Indies-Up-Side-Down-Naked-Fire-Dancing-With-Cats within 500 miles to come and do a workshop. You just need to find folks in your area, or folks who are willing to come to your area, who can teach something besides Wicca 101. You want people from a great many different paths to attend and people who have not chosen a path yet, and you want them all to feel welcome. So you need to offer them something good.

With this kind of a festival, scheduling is detailed (read "anal-retentive"), and it is a good idea to have a program printed that is handed out at the front gate where the festival folk arrive and sign in. This program can also include bios on the Big-Nose Pagans, a map of the site and directions to the closest civilization. Our program also includes the rules of conduct for the festival. At our registration gate, we have handouts from other groups, any special events during the festival, meetings, etc. Everything that is going on at the festival is put into the hands of each festivalgoer, and they are encouraged to attend as many different things as possible. We also include flyers about other events that will be happening in the future.

If you want to successfully include everyone and make them feel less shy about participating, you need a central meeting point. Find a spot that is central to your camp layout where virtually everyone will visit in the normal course of the day or maybe several times a day. This central point will give folks a place to hang out and will also provide the opportunity to meet most everyone at the festival. It also gives you a place to post notices for changes in schedule and other news. At PUF we have a central gathering point that consists of an open-sided tent, a couple of picnic tables, a trashcan and lights. It is very simple, nothing fancy, but it meets our needs. It sits right in the middle of the merchant row, which is set up in a long horseshoe arrangement. This gathering point is a place where folks can sit and talk, rest while shopping, play music, get out of the rain and just socialize. It has a very informal air to it, and so newbies are not over-awed to walk up and talk to a Big-Nose Pagan. It has been dubbed "the place where the VIPs hold court". Think about it—if an author is sitting at a picnic table talking to a dozen or so people who are standing, sitting at the table, on the table or on the ground, this does not look like a private meeting. It looks and is casual, and it is not intimidating in any way. People feel comfortable just walking up and hanging out too. It works to make people feel that they are an important part of the festival and that they are being welcomed with open arms. It also brings folks to the merchant row where they might buy something, and that makes the merchants happy as well. It also makes the merchants feel they are a part of the festival. Too often they never get out of the merchant row, and with this setup they get to socialize as well as work.

We also post notices at this gathering point because sooner or later everyone comes through this area. Communication is important, especially when things can change from moment to moment because of unforeseen circumstances. I cannot stress too heavily the importance of a central meeting place if you want a "this festival is for everyone" atmosphere at your event.

In the normal course of events, folks have a tendency to gravitate toward their own, and so the Wiccans will hang out with the Wiccans, the Druids with the other Druids and so forth. Without a central meeting spot, there might not be much mixing. Folks won't be able to meet a lot of other folks except at the workshops, rituals and meals. These are times when most folks will be busy with the business at hand, not meeting and greeting. The different trads will probably want to camp together or rent cabins that are together, so they can socialize. Some people will not feel comfortable going to someone else's encampment uninvited. We don't have that problem at PUF. There is a party circuit, and people visit the Druids, and then may amble over to check on what the Heathens are up to, or hang out with the Wiccans. Everyone is welcome and encouraged to visit. You may not be so fortunate. Keep in mind that you will have some folks who attend solo; your job is to make these people feel welcome and part of the festival. Otherwise they will feel isolated, they won't have a good time, and they will not be back. And they will tell others.

At our first festival, I had not thought about the mixing and mingling thing. I figured that a lot of the folks attending would know others at the festival, and they would all just hang out. You know, the Pagan equivalent of "If you build it they will come." We had a bonfire, and some folks gathered around that and sang, talked and visited after ritual. Since it was a bunch of Pagans, someone turned up with a guitar. A few folks brought drums and they played along. As I walked around the site, I noticed that not everyone was at the bonfire; many people were sitting around in small groups doing nothing and looking bored. At that point it dawned on me that I had not given much thought to the social aspect of the festival. I guess I thought that folks would turn up and just naturally fall into conversations with each other. Well, many of the folks attending were solitary or from different covens, and they were not doing such a good job of mingling. My heart sank. The staff had a quick conference, and we decided that we would encourage folks to mingle. My thugs went out with orders to drag people down to the bonfire so that everyone could meet everyone else. It took some effort, a little poking, a little prodding and even a little threatening, but it worked. Most of the people who attended that first year spent hours around the fire making new friends, greeting old ones and having a great time. But it took real effort. Herding cats is a tough, sweaty business. You can avoid this problem by creating a central meeting point, even if it is only a big tree in the middle of the site. Dress it up in some way so that people will know it is a meeting point, and encourage people to go there and hang out. Sooner or later, folks will get the idea.

If the site you choose has a mess hall, this is a good place for a central meeting point too. The only problem is traffic, and as your festival gets bigger, you will have to deal with it. The site that we use now has a mess hall which also houses the kitchen. We also set classes up in that hall. It has a large covered porch, and everyone loves to gather on that porch. It is a perfect place for that. The first couple of years that we used the site, this worked out ok. But as the festival got larger, there were too many people and too much traffic in and out of the main hall for it to continue to work well. Between meal preparation, classes in the hall and everyone coming and going, it became a huge traffic problem. The folks gathered on the porch had to be called down constantly because they disturbed the folks in the class. Then we had to throw them all off the porch so the dinner line could form. Many of them left their personal paraphernalia behind. It was a regular goat screw. So we moved the meeting place to merchant row, and it works well for us.

We also have two bonfire areas where dancing, drumming and chanting takes place. Almost everyone comes to one bonfire or the other before the night is done, sometimes both. So, lots of visiting goes on. For the past several years, we have had a Guedra at the bonfire on at least one night of the festival. Many people from all trads attend, either to participate or just to watch. It is a very cool experience, and it certainly brings folks together. For those of you who don't know, Guedra is Moroccan trance dancing, the whirling dervishes. Very cool.

Some festivals use the "we are all in this together" idea and also set up the camping areas according to special interest groups. So you will find an area for bards, tarot readers, Asatru and so on. There may also be informal workshops on a variety of interests. Some even set up areas for families with children, and there can be discussion groups between parents about the difficulties of raising Pagan children. This also allows people who do not have children and don't want to be bothered by them to camp in a different area. Many people think that you get the best of both worlds with this set-up; a large "everyone is welcome" group, but you also have places where folks with particular interests can gather.

There are many festivals that cater to the needs of specific groups or kinds of groups. These include a single tradition that has different branches, covens and sister covens, Druids, Asatru, Anglo-Saxon Heathens, Radical Fairies, Dianic groups, Reclaiming and so forth. These specific gatherings are usually small and have a family-like atmosphere. Many, if not most, of the festival folk know one another, which creates a nice comfort zone. This makes for a very relaxed festival, where most of the folks attending pitch in with everything from food to workshops. The workshops are chosen to educate and enlighten a particular group. All the activities and rituals are of that specific group or tradition. This can be a fairly easy festival to pull off. If you are the member of a particular group or tradition, then you are in communication with others of like mind. So you should know what and whom the folks attending are interested in seeing and activities in which they would like to participate. The ritual part of this type of festival can be planned easily with no arguments. Okay, so these are Pagans we are talking about…how about it can be planned with no arguments most of the time…alright, alright, a minimum of arguments then.

Some festivals are designed around a theme or subject. At some of these festivals the theme is only truly evident in some of the workshops and a guest or two and in the main ritual. You know the idea is there, but you are not beaten to death with it. Now some festivals are very serious about a theme and only allow workshops and rituals that are concerned with the chosen theme. The danger here is that this type of a festival may lose a large number of potential festival folk if the subject does not appeal over a wide range. For example, we have discussed having all the workshops at PUF pertain to some facet of ritual construction. We thought about constructing the classes so that the students would be the folks who would actually perform the rituals during the festival. We have done this on a small scale in the past. Isaac Bonewits has taught ritual construction workshops, and the class attendees performed the main ritual, and that worked very well. There are many places to go with this theme, but finally we thought it was too narrow and decided against doing it. We still have many classes on ritual; "Ritual Construction," "Newbies in Ritual," "Rituals for Large Groups," etc. But we also have lots of other types of classes as well so that everyone can find something they like.

While we are on this chapter, let's talk about "clothing optional" and what that means. "Clothing optional" means that folks don't have to wear clothes unless they want to, or they can wear as little as possible and any combination in between. There are many festivals where this is standard operating procedure. If you don't like that idea, there are a couple of different ways for you to handle this issue. First, you can say that clothing is not an option, and make sure that people understand that and comply with it. You will have people bitch at you, but stick to your guns. We are a "Keep Your Clothes On" festival. We have several reasons for our policy, such as simply good taste (and the danger of having our retinas burned out), the danger of sunburn, we are in a state park and the rangers would flip out, and the way the laws are written in our state we could get in lots of hot water. Plus, I personally do not want to deal with the controversy.

Another way to handle the "clothing" issue is to have a clothing-optional site, and make sure that you spell that out in the information that you hand out. Make sure that people understand that there will be folks at your festival walking around in the all together. Since many people do not read the fine print, make sure this is spelled out in BIG LETTERS.

The third way to handle this is to set aside a certain area of your site as "Clothing-Optional Land." Again spell it out; this area is for folks to be naked if they wish. Put up a sign on the site so that folks will know that they are entering Clothing-Optional Land, and there will be no silly misunderstandings. Make sure that people who want this option understand that they must don clothing to wander the rest of the site.

Before you decide on the clothing or no clothing issue, you might want to check your local and state laws about naked adults being in the presence of minors. The last thing you want is to make the 10:00 News.

There are a lot of festivals now, as compared to when we started out, and they are all different. This is because the people that put them on are different and have their own ideas about how a festival needs to be run. Put your own fertile imagination to work on this issue. What do you like? Ask other members of your community what interests them. Ask people whom they would like to see as guests. Go to where the Pagans are and get your info. Get input, and then put it all together.

The first PUF was a one-day only event. This got our feet wet, and showed us how much we knew and how much we didn't. I reasoned that all of the mistakes we made in planning would only have to be endured from sun up to sun down, and everyone involved would probably survive. I claim that this one idea proves I am not crazy (at least about that). I really suggest this idea for all first-timers. Start small and build your numbers, and you will find the going much easier for you.

For me, the bottom line for a festival is that it should allow the festival folks who attend (and you) to connect with the Divine. It should be positive and life-affirming. You want folks to leave at the end of the weekend energized and ready to take their great feelings and information back to their community. At the end of the day, this is all about *faith*.

Getting Help
Ask and ye shall receive.

The first thing that you need to know is, you are not doing this in a vacuum. Let me say that again, YOU ARE NOT DOING THIS IN A VACUUM!!! I see people trying to pull off a festival, or a Pagan Pride Day or a workshop with a Big-Nose Pagan, and they try to do it all by themselves. That is just stupid. For the love of gods, reach out into the community and find some people to help you. There might be some folks in your area that know a thing or two about what you are trying to do. They may have contacts that you do not have yet. They may just know more people than you know. Use that knowledge. Your event will be a better success, people in the community will have warm and fuzzy feelings toward you, and you will not make yourself crazy trying to do it all.

When we started down this road, we were novices. We had decided to have a festival, and then we all stood around scratching our heads and saying "Now what?" The first thing we did was to look at ourselves and take stock of the talents we possessed. We found out, much to our own amazement, that we had quite a lot. But we did not have enough to pull off a festival all by ourselves.

Thankfully, we were smart enough to know that we needed to ask others for help, and we were not too proud to do it. Surely, we reasoned, someone somewhere had to know how to throw a really big party. So we started looking.

We went to other covens in the area and begged for help. We told them that we wanted to do this crazy thing, and we needed help finding teachers for the classes, spreading the word about the festival and doing all the actual work on-site. Several of the local groups stepped up to the plate, for which I am grateful. Every coven has members that are experts in some field. Ask them to recommend a member to teach; many of them will be flattered that you asked.

After I had pitched the idea of a festival to some of the local Pagans, I started searching for a perfect place to hold the festival. There were several requirements that I felt we needed; it had to have a fair amount of open land, it had to be private, and it had to be cheap. I did not have a lot of luck at first. Finally, I put the entire venture into the hands of the God and Goddess. I figured if They wanted to see Tennessee Pagans playing in the woods, They would open the doors for me. I also put the word out on the Pagan grapevine. Funny thing how prayer is answered because it was not long before the priestess of another local coven, Oak, Ash and Thorn, came to my rescue. She knew of a place that only cost $50 to rent for a whole day!

I asked the leaders of Oak, Ash and Thorn to join with my group so that we could do the ritual together. There were some logistics to work out, and while there were some glaring differences in style, it went well and folks had a good time. I really felt that it was a good example of cooperation between Pagans.

Blake from Tangled Moon built a labyrinth in the field next to the ritual field. He laid it out with flour. Starhelm from Oak, Ash and Thorn built one with deadfall. In fact, labyrinth building was an actual class, so there were a lot of folks to help them. Many people spent the morning dragging deadfall from the woods and setting it into a labyrinth pattern.

The next year, I decided to put the festival in the hands of a local organization called S.P.I.R.A.L., which stands for Serving Pagans in Religion and Life. The reasons for doing this were twofold. It would give us more hands to help run the festival. It would also take the festival into a bigger arena and make it the work of many people, not just one group with one or two other groups pitching in to help. Pagan politics being what they are, it seemed like a good idea. It worked out very well for us. So, look and see if there are any organized groups in your area, not just covens.

The year that we decided to expand our festival to a weekend event, we found the perfect park in which to hold it. There was just one little problem; someone had already booked it for the weekend we wanted. So we inquired as to the person's name and were surprised to find out that the person was a Pagan from just outside of Nashville, one Lady Morgaine. We contacted her and found out that she wanted to put on a festival and had booked the park. She was new to the area and did not realize that there was already one festival in progress. We suggested that we join forces since she had the park and we had the organization. She agreed and we hijacked her reservations. A fine example of cooperation.

Getting Help

We are fortunate to have our very own Big-Nose Pagan in this neck of the woods named Grey Cat. She has written several books and is very familiar with the Pagan festival circuit. We invited her, and she agreed to come play with us. She has taught Ritual 101 classes that explained the etiquette of doing ritual with others and how to behave. We thought it was a class that was very necessary since we had solitaries and so many people new to the path attending. She has also taught other classes and performed several rituals over the years.

So start with the Pagans in your area that you know. Many of them will step up to the plate; you just have to be brave enough to ask. True, some will turn you down, but don't allow yourself to be discouraged. Work with the ones that will work with you, and remember that when they come knocking on your door, you owe them. Despite what you may think or have heard or even experienced, it really is possible for Pagans to work together. Our festival is living proof of that.

Don't be afraid to go outside the Pagan community to find help. You will be amazed at what you will find. Several members of our coven were involved with the Society of Creative Anachronisms, a worldwide historical reenactment organization. True, our aims are different. Their events include people in funny clothes who like to hit each other with sticks while living in an altered zone of time and space. Our events involve people in funny clothes running around with sharp pointy things while living in an altered zone of time and space; we just try not to hit anyone. (Hey wait a minute! That sounds very similar!) Actually, there are huge differences; they recreate history and we deal with spirituality. But they also know how to camp, cook for large groups of hungry people and present great workshops to entertain and enlighten. And they are damn good at it.

We started to ask questions about places to hold events, how to cook for a large group of people and still have it taste good, how to figure out how much food to buy, length of class-time, in short, all of the logistics for handling people. Before too long, all of our SCA friends began to get that "deer in the headlights" look whenever they saw any of us coming with more questions. But we just smiled and asked our questions anyway. (We did find that plying them with alcohol helped to ease their pain.) Luckily, a couple of us had actually done the cooking for several SCA events and could draw on that experience. After a few months of gathering facts and figures from our friends, and adding our own scant knowledge to the mix, we felt a little more prepared to actually throw an event ourselves. But only a little. Facts and figures on paper are a long way from actual people running loose in the woods. We knew that.

The first year, the funds for the festival came out of my own pocket, which was pretty thin. So, I looked for ways to defray that cost. I put the word out that we needed help with food. Within a week, a woman approached me to tell me that a friend of a friend of hers worked at a bagel place that did not sell their day old bagels. They went into the trash. The manager was delighted to donate all the day old bagels to us since he felt bad about just throwing them away. We picked up garbage bags full of bagels for three days before the festival—lots and lots of bagels. Neither the woman who worked at the bagel place nor the manager was Pagan, but they had no qualms about giving us bagels. In return, we told all the Pagans in town where the bagels had come from and encouraged them to shop there.

In my ramblings, I had the good fortune to meet a man named Tony Kail who is an occult crimes investigator. He presents workshops for law enforcement groups, and because of his expertise, he has been called into police investigations many times. He called me to ask a few questions that were pertinent to an investigation he was working on. I was very impressed with his knowledge of the occult and religious practices, even the obscure ones. So I called him and asked if he would be willing to come to our festival and present a workshop. He agreed and became our first headliner. Tony is a non-Pagan but is Pagan-friendly enough to come play in the woods with us. He is a brave fellow as well as a knowledgeable one.

You have to be determined to have people and entertainment at your festival that is top-notch. To do this you must become an unabashed self-promoter. You must be willing to ask anyone you think will add to your festival to come and be a part of it. You must not be shy. So what if you get turned down a time or two, what is the worse thing that can happen? Will it kill you? Nope, it will not. I promise that you will get more "yes" than "no" answers from the people you approach.

The really good news is that as your festival grows larger and becomes better known, you won't have to beat the bushes so hard to find

Getting Help

people who are willing to be a part of your festival. They will find you. As we have become better known, groups have approached us. One year a Pagan women's group wanted to have an ice cream social to raise money for fire fighting equipment to replace what was lost by the New York City Fire Department on 9/11. That was a good cause, and we agreed to let them hold their event. (Besides, ice cream is always high on my personal list.) As we had no official lunch period that year, the ice cream social took place during the breaks in the afternoon. The women's group took care of finding ice cream donors and hauling all of it to the site. They ended up getting Baskin and Robbins—yum. This was a win-win situation for everyone; us, festivalgoers, the women's group and the fire department of New York City. As we have gotten larger, we have had many musical groups and individuals contact us about entertaining at PUF, and merchants and workshop facilitators as well.

There are a lot of people right in your own back yard that will be willing to help you with your festival, Pagan and non-Pagan alike. All you have to do is go and stalk…I mean hunt them, and place your request before them. Many will cooperate. Have faith.

Setting up the labyrinth

⊰**Staff**⊱
Who you gonna call?

First, you have to have dedicated people to help you run a festival because it is a lot of hard work. The details will kill you, and there will be a hundred things that you did not think of before they sneak up and bite you on the ass.

I am very lucky. To put the pieces together for our first festival I went to the members of my group, Witches of the Woods, and discussed the crazy idea with them. They are a bunch of folks who have a lot of different talents. So I had a good base with which to work.

The second year, I joined forces with a local Pagan group, S.P.I.R.A.L. and that brought more hands to help. Good thing too; we had more folks the second year, and more people means more work. Over the years, the core of my staff has been my own group, but we have reached out into the community for more numbers. No choice—our festival has grown from ninety-seven attendees to 426. The amount of work needed to make it happen has grown as well.

Many people have come to me over the years to volunteer for staff positions, and if I knew them or they came highly recommended to me, I have taken them on board. Sometimes this approach has worked, and sometimes not. A staff position means free admission to the festival. There have been those who only volunteer in order to get a free ride. What they find out is there really is no such thing as a free lunch. That should be our motto, TINSTAAFL. They must work hard for it.

This staff business is a fine line to walk; you must have people who are willing to work hard, who have the patience of Job, who have a good sense of humor and take their fun where they find it. They must also have their heads screwed on fairly tightly, be able to stand up to people who try to push them around, be firm when necessary and be fair in the extreme. You must find people who believe in the dream as much as you do and are willing to work like indentured servants to pull it off.

They must not bitch at being overworked, piss off the festival folk with a bad attitude nor hide in the woods to get out of work. All of these things have occurred at PUF. It is annoying in the extreme to have to hunt staff members down to get them to do the work at hand or apologize to everyone they piss off on site. Every year, I pay attention to the staff members and observe how they go about their assigned tasks. And every year, I cull the staff and find replacements. I have been accused of being unfair, of being a slave driver and of only picking "my own people." I don't think that I am unfair; I work as hard or harder than any member on the staff. I do rely on my own folks first; they have proven their worth over the years. A festival organizer must have people on whom he/she can place total trust. A huge pack of folks have risen up to be added to the staff of PUF who are not "my people" but are people who want to see this event continue and be the best festival around. I can only hope that you are as lucky as I have been over the years.

Our staff at this point consists of about twenty-five folks, give or take. There are some changes from year to year, but it has remained fairly consistent for the past several years. Here is the breakdown:

Festival Coordinator - Chief cook and bottle washer. This is the position that calls all the shots, makes all the hard decisions, picks the staff, fires the staff, cracks heads, puts out fires, takes all the blame, takes up everyone's slack, does all the worrying, loses sleep, has fantasies of robbing banks for the needed funds and begins to take on a haunted look about six weeks before the event. True, there is a staff to lean on, but in the final analysis, the buck stops right here. The Festival Coordinator will have to have amazing reserves of energy and a very thick skin to take on this position. He/she cannot take himself or herself too seriously and must have a good sense of humor. This is the person everyone will come to for answers. They had better have some.

Reservation God/Goddess - If you allow folks to buy tickets prior to your event, you have to keep good records. You have to know who has paid and who has not. You also have to know how many people are coming and where they are all going to sleep. This is not such a problem if you have a camping only event, but if you are selling beds, your counts must be accurate. You sell the same bed twice, and you have a real problem. This is the person who will take care of the money (unless you choose a treasurer) and will tell you how much money you have to spend. You need someone with good organizational skills for this position.

Security Thug - A good security chief is mild mannered, has good people skills, can think on his/her feet and has the ability to defuse a potentially ugly situation with grace and charm. Don't pick a real thug. This is a position that requires finesse not muscles. This is also the person who will make a schedule for security rounds and will pick the people to make those rounds. So, he/she has to be a good judge of character as well. Remember this is the person in whom every person attending your festival will place his or her trust. Everyone who comes to your festival must know that they will be protected and their belongings as well. You have to trust him/her totally.

Kitchen Witch - If you intend to provide food, even if it is only one meal, you need someone you have faith in for this job. A festival, like an army, runs on its belly; you will be dealing with some really hungry folks. Believe it or not, folks will remember if the food was lousy even if the rest of the event was great. And they will tell others. If the food is good, they will sing your praises and make comments about you on their websites. FOOD IS IMPORTANT!!! The person in this position must be a good cook, be able to cook for large numbers of folks, know how to find a bargain and buy the food while staying on a budget. Pick someone who has done this before. Never let an inexperienced person run your kitchen; you are courting disaster.

Workshop Guru - You need someone with good people skills for this position. He/she will have to deal with folks that, in many cases, have large egos. You need someone who can be diplomatic while turning someone down for a workshop. This person must have a good working knowledge of many different trads so that correct decisions can be made about teachers and workshops. This is the person who will set the schedule for the workshops, and that is a nightmare. He/she must also work to accommodate everyone who is teaching, if possible. This is also the person who must squirrel around to find a replacement class when someone drops out at the last minute, so a modicum of calmness is required.

VIP Wrangler - If you have Big-Nose Pagans at your events, someone must take care of them. If they are traveling some distance, directions must be given or planes and trains met. This really is the person who goes to the airport and holds up a sign with "XYZ Festival" written on it, just like in the movies. This is also the person who communicates with the VIP or their handler and makes all the arrangements. If your guests are flying in or taking a train, they will not be able to bring camping gear with them, some must be provided. They must also be taken back to the airport or train station at the end of the festival. At PUF we like to treat our VIPs special, we want them to have a good experience so that they will come back. I am assured that we do a good job in this area.

Merchant Manager - This is the person who must deal with the merchants, find out how much space they need, what they will be bringing, if they require electricity, and if they will be camping with their wares or will need other accommodations. This person needs to understand merchants, so it is wise to pick someone who is a merchant. Merchants are a touchy lot (I can say that 'cause I am one) and need special handling. You want to keep your merchants happy; they are a big draw for your festival. By the same token, you cannot let them run all over you either—and they will because they are a hardheaded, stubborn, take-charge bunch of folks. They have to be in order to make a living at this crazy game.

Kid Herder - If you are crazy enough to tackle this, you need someone who has training. You cannot put a novice in this job; the kids will turn on him/her and eat such a person for lunch. You know I am right. So pick someone who is a combination school teacher/drill sergeant. He/she needs to have organizational skills and the imagination to engage children. This person has to like children but must be firm with them too.

Camp Crier - This person makes the rounds of the camp on a regular basis to tell people about classes, lunch, dinner, ritual and other regular events. This person has to pay attention to the schedule and the clock so that the events can be cried in a timely fashion. You don't want to have to go and find your crier to remind them to do their job, so you need someone who is responsible.

Teen Tuner - I know it is a silly name, but work with me here. This is the person who thinks up activities for the teens so that they will have lots of things to do and will feel that they are a part of the festival.

There are other coordinators that you might want to add at your discretion or at your need: Front Gate Marshal, Entertainment Coordinator and maybe someone to urge folks to participate in activities—a Social Director, as it were. At PUF all the staff members are social directors and look for folks that are not participating and encourage them to do so. We drag people around and introduce them and make sure no one eats meals alone. We are a fairly pushy lot. We have to be.

We have been doing this for a few years, and I like to think that we have fine-tuned it pretty well. But of course I like to think that I can do all the things now that I could do at thirty. So I may be a bit deluded. I hope that you can find people to work with who can read your mind and smack you in the head when you need it, like I have. It helps.

The rest of the staff members fill in where they are needed, and they relieve anyone who needs a break. In short, the staff members without titles are the ones who do everyone's job. So every member of your staff must understand the logistics of all the jobs.

You must be sure and pick staff members that have a good concept of the "team player" mentality and that you think can work and play well with others. Your staff will spend a lot of time together in the months leading up to the festival and will actually live in each other's hip pockets the week of festival. You also have to pick staff members that will be able to take the time off from work in order to be at the festival for the entire time, front to back.

There must be staff meetings so that everyone is on the same page. You will want to organize meetings so that all of your staff members can attend. At these meetings everyone can discuss the plans for the festival. This is the time that everyone can throw in their two cents worth, make suggestions, bitch about things and talk about how to fine-tune ideas. You want to listen to your staff; after all, you picked them for their brains as well as their strong backs. You can run it like a board with you as the CEO, or a democracy or a dictatorship. Your choice. I choose to run it like a board, but I have veto power, and the final buck always stops with me. So I guess that makes it a benevolent dictatorship. Have I pissed off members of my own staff in the past? Have people quit because they did not like the way I ran my island? You betcha, and it probably will happen in the future as well.

We have meetings months in advance to discuss what needs to be done and how to do it. We sit down and really look at the problems from the year before. Yes, we have a list of them because we ask the members of the staff to contribute any and all problems they see. I keep a notebook that is reserved for PUF stuff, and I save my notes from year to year, so baby, we have plenty of lists. There are always several problems from the year before, and we tackle them early. We discuss plane reservations, entertainment, space, theme and a hundred other things in these meetings. We also have a group mail so that every communication goes to the entire staff. That cuts down on the wear and tear of having to answer lots of emails from the staff or trying to get one staff member in touch with another. Very simple.

I also set meetings with all my "department heads" separately from the large staff meetings. At these meetings we discuss specifics about their area. Sometimes I drag in other staff members into these discussions as well. We are just meeting fools.

Some staff positions require items to be bought for the festival, such as the food, the kid's stuff, PR announcements such as flyers and so on. You must keep a tight rein on the purse strings. People tend to be very single minded and only look at their own area, not at the entire picture. In which case, they may not be too frugal with the money they are spending. You need to keep the checkbook, and let folks go out and find the items they need and then check in with you to discuss the cost. If you give your staff free rein to buy what they think the festival needs, you will find yourself spending lots of money for things that are cute or funny but that you can do without. Plan out a budget for each area of the festival. With a budget you can say things like, "I know the furry house shoes with little witch hats on top would be great for all the VIP's and are really cute, but there is not enough money in the budget to allow you to spend $27 a piece on them." See how well that works!

You will sometimes find that your staff members are jealous of their positions and do not like the idea of someone stepping on their toes by invading what they consider their territory. Reassure them that their position is important and their contribution is of great value, but this is a team effort. If you really see a situation where someone is usurping another's role, step in and nip that in the proverbial bud. If you find yourself with a staff member who simply cannot get along with the others or who continually seeks to steal the limelight, give them their walking papers. This may be a difficult choice to make, and you may actually lose a friend over it, but it will make your life much more pleasant in the long run.

Unfortunately, most of the real problems with staff usually do not become apparent until the actual festival, and then you are more or less stuck. In that case, try and keep the peace, or clean up the mess, and just keep on going. I have had staff members that tried to duck work, had bad attitudes and whined, a lot. You can live with all of that. Unfortunately, one year I had a staff member that was a real problem. This person was rude to the festival folks and, in short, acted as if being a member of staff was some kind of a power position. Man, did I have complaints that year! I tried to soothe the situation over and confronted the staff member. It did not stop. I guess I could have killed the individual and thrown her in the lake, but instead I spent a lot of time trying to sooth ruffled feathers.

After the festival, I even got emails from people who swore they would never come back to PUF because of this one person's behavior. I hated that and sent an email of apology and reassurance that the situation had been corrected and that the staff member in question had been removed from staff. Then I quietly removed the name from my staff list. There was no confrontation, I just did not contact the person the next year—nor was I contacted. Problem solved. Of course sometimes it is not that easy to fire someone, and there is a firefight over it. Too bad—you have to do whatever you need to do to keep your festival healthy.

Live and learn, and hand out the pink slips where you need to. You may be plagued with a bad staff member during the festival, but you can tuck yourself in at night with this delightful thought. You will not have to deal with complaints and woes because of that staff member next year. And always remember that murder is illegal.

ೞOrganizationಲ
How anal-retentive are you?

How organized do you want to be? That depends on what kind of a person you are. Must all the *i*'s be dotted and the *t*'s crossed in your world, or do you like flying by the seat of your pants? It is a serious question, and only you can answer it.

Some festivals are very free and loose and have just enough organization to allow the festival to happen and not float away into the ether. These festivals allow the freedom for each person attending to more or less design their own festival. Some classes are scheduled, but anyone attending the festival may decide to offer a class and can post the information about the class, the time and location on a bulletin board, and if anyone is interested they will attend. Tents are set up in a designated area, but people can group them together in whatever manner they wish. Many of these festivals have a pay at the door policy. Food may be a combination of potluck that the festival folk bring to contribute. Some have vendors that sell food; some festivals ask that you bring your own food and drink. This kind of festival offers an opportunity for folks to get together, hang out and go to workshops if they want, and just generally visit and have a good time. There is usually no written program handed out, as the schedule is subject to change. They are laid-back, dude.

Now we are very organized, as you may have guessed. A triple Virgo runs PUF, and we have lots of Virgos in training. That should tell you all you need to know. We post all the activities for each day at the front gate and on the front door of the main hall. We have several areas set aside for workshops, and we post all the workshops that will take place that day at each area. We have a printed program that everyone receives at the front gate when they sign in. We cry the entire camp before each workshop as well as before lunch, dinner and rituals. This way no one misses anything in which they really want to participate. We also do this because sometimes we have changes in scheduling, and we want everyone to be informed.

We encourage pre-registration so that we have some idea how many people will be attending. This gives us a working idea of how much food, drink and toilet paper to buy. When we get a final gate count each day, we may have to send someone to the store for some extras, but they won't have to buy too much. It also gives us money to buy the items we need up front.

We put all our tent campers in one area and set them up in an organized fashion along rows or streets. We lay out ten or twelve tent spaces from the main road in a horseshoe design. This leaves an open space in the middle so that the folks on that "street" can have a gathering area. Then we move over and lay out another "street." Yes, we use little flags to keep it all straight. I have spent hours in the rain laying out the streets for our camping area and pushing little flags into the ground. I passed over areas that were soggy from the rain, and no one had to sleep in a puddle. So, as anal-retentive as it sounds, there are good solid reasons why we do it this way, and it is not just for the sake of my triple Virgo-ness. On the street plan, everyone knows where to put their tent so that they do not set it on top of someone else (a common complaint before we adopted this system). All of the doors of the tents on every street all face into the open space, and in case of a problem, there is a clear and open avenue to get out of the tents and into the main road without tripping over tent stakes and ropes. This is great, not just in the case of an emergency, but also keeps accidents down when folks wander to the bathroom late at night. And no one sleeps in a puddle, most of the time. Ok, we even laugh at ourselves over this major bit of anal-retentiveness, but it works.

We have children's activities so that parents can go to class, and the kids can play and have a good time too. It is the one area that we have tweaked and tweaked, and it is still (as of this writing) not what we want it to be. I like to think of it as a work in progress, which makes me feel somewhat better about the whole thing.

We ask everyone attending, except merchants, to volunteer 1.5 hours over the weekend to work. We call it Community Service. We have played with that over the years and now have created a schedule for work shifts, assigning folks to jobs that need to be done throughout the day. The work shifts are in 1.5 hour blocks, and those run at the same time as the classes. And yes, people do bitch about it. We just explain to them that we could not pull the festival off without them. And that's true; a festival is just too much work for only a few folks. But people like to feel needed, so telling them we need them gets us much better cooperation.

We put ID bracelets on everyone, and they are specific colors to indicate the number of days a person will be on site. We also have one for the kids that is actually a medical ID bracelet that has a clear window in which you slip a piece of paper with all the child's info. That way, lost kids can be returned to their parents. Everyone under 18 wears one of these. We require that everyone keep his or her bracelet on at all times. The little kids usually have to have an ID bracelet placed around an ankle since they tend to slip off their skinny little wrists.

We also have a list of rules. And people bitch about that too. Believe me, every one of the rules on our list is for a good reason. And every year, we usually add one more because the year before someone does something stupid that we had not thought anyone would do.

Many festivals are as organized as PUF, and some even more so. The bigger the festival, the more organization it needs. You are trying to herd a lot of people, keep them safe, feed them and still let them have a good time. Pagan Spirit Gathering is very organized. They too have folks from all paths, and the organizers try to have something for everyone. They have a "town meeting" every morning for announcements about what will be happening and any changes to the schedule. We have not implemented that yet, but we intend to do so. They also have a program they hand out to their festival folk. It looks like a newspaper.

We start planning our next festival as soon as we recover from the one we just did. I feel that the more organized you are, there will be less to go wrong come the actual festival. Truthfully, no matter how well you plan, there will be things that you forget or that go wrong. The weather will suck, class facilitators will fail to show, someone will be allergic to the soap. That is just a part of the human condition. All of those things and more have happened to us, but we have developed a back-up plan for almost everything. Good planning with attention to detail will keep the annoying moments from becoming tragic moments. You are dealing with human beings; think of all the things that can go wrong and plan accordingly.

Most festivals fall somewhere in between "Anally organized to within an inch of its life" and "We just let what needs to happen, happen." You get to choose what kind of a festival you want to have based on your comfort level. Remember this; you can start out with a free form festival and move to a more organized festival as your festival grows. So you don't have to be obsessive-compulsive to begin with unless, like some of us, you just can't help yourself.

Registration tents at the main gate

⌘Festival Site☙
Do not try this at home!

Finding a place to hold the festival might be the most difficult part of the equation. First you have to decide on the geography for your festival, and there are several kinds. Of course, the perfect idea is to own the land yourself; you can do what you want, when you want and in whatever manner you want. But there is a whole different set of headaches with that. Regardless of the pros and cons, most of us do not own a large piece of land or anything else that is suitable for a festival, so we have to rent. Depending on where you live, you may run into the problem of folks who do not want to rent to you because of the nature of the festival. Pagans still have a bad name in many parts of the country.

Let's start with indoor festivals; these are usually held at hotels. This type of festival has a lot going for it. It is indoors, so you are not bothered by nature. (Only kidding.) But it will not be too hot or too cold, and it won't matter if it rains cats and dogs, or you get a freak snowstorm in April and there will not be MUD. (Oh, but I am not bitter about any of those things!) You will even have cable television and ice machines. There might be a pool. You will not be bug-bitten or sunburned either. You will get to sleep on a real bed. Ah, all the comforts of home. Plus, you and your staff will not have to work so hard during the weekend. There is maid service. All things considered, this is not a bad way to go. But, read on before you decide.

The down side to a hotel festival is that it is indoors, and some folks may find it difficult to connect to nature through all that concrete. Also, you will have to behave in a manner that will not scare the other guests or the management and get you kicked to the curb. While we are on the subject of other guests, unless you have enough folks to fill all the rooms in your chosen hotel, you will be mixing with the "muggles."

The costs will be greater with a hotel festival as well. The meeting rooms will have a price tag; so will the ballroom if you use one. Most hotels do not let you bring in your own food or drink either. They will want to cater the food. They will charge you for pitchers of ice water and tea and coffee. That alone will drive the cost up. You will have to pass the costs along to your festival folks, many of whom will be staying at the hotel for the weekend, and they will have a room rental fee as well. You may also have to contend with the headache of booking a block of rooms and trying to fill them. Many hotels will want you to be responsible for the cost of any rooms you book even if they do not sell.

Next, you have group camps. Try looking at resorts, private camps and state parks. This is a nice compromise between hotels and really roughing it. On the plus side, you will be out in nature. You will also probably not have to share the space with non-Pagans. Many times, these camps have large meeting halls and an industrial-strength kitchen. Both wonderful things for your festival. Some have buildings where everyone can sleep, some have separate cabins and some only have tenting. The cost for this kind of event will be much lower than in a hotel. Shop around until you find the camp with the best price, the best accommodations and one that will fit the size of your festival. Don't be afraid to approach the church camps; many of them will rent to groups outside of their religion. They have bills to pay too. See if there is a Boy Scout or Girl Scout camp in the area, and ask if they rent to outside groups. You have more options with this idea than you might think.

Most festivals as of this writing are using primitive sites. The name means exactly what you think it means. They are usually held on private land and only have fields to tent camp, a fire pit for cooking and latrines; you may even have to haul your own water. Here you are going to really be in touch with nature. There are some great festivals that operate on primitive sites. In some parts of the country, there are primitive, privately owned campsites that will lease their property to folks who need space to run a festival. Some primitive sites are not so primitive and have buildings, a kitchen, some modern plumbing and a bit of electricity. If this is the idea you run with, find out what the site has in the way of civilization, if any. Is there running water, plumbing, flush toilets, electricity? If you are using a site that has latrines, make sure you ask how deep they are and if there will be lime or something comparable to toss into them occasionally as the weekend progresses. Even if you have to bring tiki torches, haul water and rent port-a-johns, you can still make a primitive site work; it just takes planning.

With any of these ideas, go and see the space that you will be renting. Don't take someone else's word for the accommodations. You should make several trips to the site to really get the lay of the land or hotel clearly in your mind. If you choose an outdoor festival, you will need a big, flat field for ritual and a place where people can put up tents. If the property is off the beaten track, so to speak, that is a bonus. It is never cool to have non-Pagans show up in the middle of your ritual. You will also want to get everything in writing; the cost of the site, the rental fees, the per-head cost if there is one on top of the rental fee, check-in time, check-out time, rules about fires, clothing (optional or not), trash disposal, food prep—in short, the entire list of rules that the site owners have drawn up for usage of their site.

Our first two festivals were held in a small, city-owned park about one hour out of Nashville. It was a great discovery! There were working bathrooms and a covered picnic area. The park itself was very beautiful with many wooded acres and open fields as well as lots of trails to hike. The city rented the park for the entire day, so we could have the place to ourselves, mostly. The hiking and riding trails were still open to the public. There was a long drive into the park and then the land opened up. The actual festival site sat about a half mile off the main road, so we had privacy. The public used the hiking and riding trails, but they did not cross the actual camp area that we used. We saw a few folks enjoying the great outdoors; we waved at them and they waved back.

The site also had a covered pavilion that was huge and was a perfect place for the kids' activities and the food setup. It was only a few steps from the bathrooms, and that was a bonus. We decided that the classes would be set up under the trees. Hey, it is a nature religion after all.

The only electricity on the site was one naked light bulb in the pavilion. Not even the bathrooms had lights. Since the site was in the country, we knew it would be really dark when the sun went down. The problem was solved when someone suggested we go to the discount store and buy tiki torches. We used a dozen lanterns on the tables in the pavilion and one for each of the bathrooms.

Fortunately for us, some of our folks lived right down the road from the park, so we commandeered their house and used it for a base of operations. We spent Friday night there, so we could get an early start the next morning. The gate was set to open at 8:00 A.M. We organized the waivers and counted the change to make sure we had enough. We also cooked; well, we really made tuna and chicken salad for lunch. We also made Glop (do you really want to know what this is?) for the kids.

The second year of the festival, I felt that we were ready to do an overnight festival. The park manager told me that the park was not really set up for overnight camping, but if we could stand it, so could they. Despite the fact that there were no showers, this site still worked well. That year we cooked the food over an open fire—hard, hot work, but the roast pig was delicious!

After the first two festivals, we felt that we were ready for a two-day festival. The little city park that we loved so much would not accommodate that without a lot of extras, mainly in the way of showers. So it was time to move on. We started looking for a place that would accommodate 150 people or more and had showers.

In this part of the world, we have been very lucky to have wonderful parks. With a little research, we found one that exactly suited our needs. This particular park was about an hour outside of Nashville and had a large group camp with 120 beds! It had cabins that slept two to four people, a few that slept even more (one cabin even had a bathroom in it and a wheel-chair ramp), a big building that held a real kitchen and dining hall, a smoke house (no more standing over a fire pit!), a covered pavilion, big fields for ritual and bigger fields to accommodate the tent campers, and last but not least, bath houses with showers! It was wonderful. A big plus was that the camp was at the end of one of the roads in the park with two gates that could be shut and one that could be locked. That solved the problem of non-Pagan folks wandering through. So we were still in the woods, but we had lots of modern conveniences to take some of the pain away.

We have used this park for the last seven festivals and will keep using it until hell freezes over. We have a good working relationship with the park officials and with the rangers. They know that we take care of the property and leave it better than when we arrived. One of the rangers actually told me that he wished everyone were like us! (I am pretty sure he did not mean "Pagan.")

☙Advertising☙
If you build it, they won't come, unless they know about it.

So you have a place, a theme, a staff and a plan. Now all you need are folks to attend. Start simple—create a flyer. Take your time and make it attractive; put everything pertinent on it. You need the name, the date, where, when, a list of activities, kid-friendly or not, clothing optional or not, food or not and the cost. You want to include enough information to get a reader's attention but not too much to overwhelm the senses. Get your ideas firmly in your head for the layout and what you want to include. Then, design or get someone to design a logo for your festival so that it stands out in the crowd.

If you are capable of designing your own flyer, more power to you. I am not. Despite the fact that this book is being typed on a computer, I am not computer literate. Ask anybody. I even have a screen saver that reads "TISH IS NOT ALLOWED TO USE THIS COMPUTER." What can I say? Some of my computer nerd friends believe themselves to be comedians. My children have even said that the fact I own a computer is one of the signs of the apocalypse. My children are smart-mouthed individuals who think they are funny.

So, if you are unfortunate like me and can't navigate a computer, beg a friend to create a flyer for you. Tell him/her what you want to include, and then get out of the way. Check with all the local copy places and see who will give you the best price on copies. If you can save a penny a copy, it adds up, so shop around. Take your flyer to the place with the best deal and spend about $100 on copies. Next, put some flyers in the local Pagan/new age/metaphysical shops in your town. Look around for coffee shops or any place where alternative folks gather. Most people who own individual shops and businesses will be more than happy to accommodate you, and many places have a bulletin board just for flyers. This method works very well to spread the word around town. It is also a great way to get the info out to the solitaries in the area. Best of all, it is cheap.

Word of mouth is a great thing too. We have been very lucky to have plenty of that. After all, when we started, it was the first large gathering in the area. It got folks talking. So contact the local groups in your area, and lay your plans out for them. I know, I know, sometimes there can be a lot of jealousy and backstabbing in the community. But I think that the folks who step up to the plate and give you a hand by telling all of their folks about your festival may pleasantly surprise you.

The second year of PUF, we discovered the true joy of advertising on the web. You can get your festival in front of a lot of people there, and much of it is free! You gotta love that. The best place in the world to start is Witchvox.com. There you will find listings for the other people in your neck of the woods. Many of the groups and covens have websites of their own and welcome information. Go to the websites and find out. You should also be able to find webrings where there are links to even more groups who may agree to let you post info. This just takes good old-fashioned legwork. Please don't spam every group you find with email—besides the fact that Witchvox frowns on that type of thing, it is rude. Instead, politely go to websites, contact the Webmaster, and ask if they would be willing to post your festival info.

Besides the contacts you will find, you can also get your festival listed on the actual Witchvox website under events. It is easy to do, just follow the directions. Witchvox is the best place for getting the word out to folks. Bless them! Just about everyone who is interested in festivals will go to Witchvox first to see what's happening in their area.

If you belong to any groups on the net, you can also post the information there if the moderator is willing. That way you hit a large number of folks with one email. If you are not sure a post will be welcome, ask. It is also a great idea to add to your post that anyone who reads it is free to post it anywhere they want. Ah, see the ripples spread.

Last but not least, in this day and age, if you are serious about having a festival, you must create a website. Let me do the math for you. The first year of our festival, we did not have a website, only flyers and word of mouth. We had ninety-seven attendees. The second year of PUF, I asked a friend to create a website for me, and we posted all the information about the festival there. We also added a list of what people needed to bring in order to be comfortable. We drafted a list of rules as well so that everyone would know what was expected of them and posted that to the website. It was a very simple site, but because of it plus the other info we sent out, word about PUF began to spread like wildfire. That year we had 125 in attendance. Another bonus of our advertising on the net was that some Pagan merchants heard about us and wanted to come and play too. That rocked! Word spread and it was all good.

The third year of PUF, we created a super website that extolled all the virtues of our festival. We added the description of the site, the great classes we offered, the delicious food we served and the fabulous experience of coming to PUF. We included the waivers so that people could download them, fill them out and mail them to us. Of course, we included a mailing address so that folks could send the waivers and money to us and thus reserve a space for themselves early. (I say we, but I did not actually do much of it; I found someone with talent to do that part. That would be Lori, a girl who knows her way around computers. I just looked over her shoulder, made "ohhh" and "ahhhh" sounds and a few simple suggestions. She did the actual work.) We asked everyone involved in our festival to post the information to all the e-groups where they were members. Because we had overnight camping that year, we put the website up even earlier than the year before to give everyone more time to get their ducks in a row. Again, we went to other websites and web rings to spread the word. We still distributed flyers all over town.

Every year since, we have improved the website. Now it has all the info, the workshops, bios of the guests, dates, fees, forms, menus and pictures of past festivals—and we are hooked up to PayPal, so they can reserve a space on the spot. We have also included pictures of the festival. Folks really like seeing the pictures of the site, the rituals, guests and folks just having fun. I feel that this has helped our attendance to grow from ninety-seven the first year to 426 last year.

We have changed how we handle the waivers too, and I think it makes the process much easier. No one has to mail in their waivers anymore. It is on the website so it can be read. We have copies of it at our front gate. When a person registers, they sign the waiver at that time.

Your VIPs will also have websites, and they will probably post the info about your festival there. If you are very lucky, after the festival they might write a favorable review about their experience. M. R. Sellars wrote the first celebrity review of PUF; of course, he mostly raved about the food, but it still made us look good. Since that time, several of our other guests have written about their experiences at PUF, and I am very grateful to them for the good PR.

If you want to make your festival more than a small local event, you have to think bigger. Every year we dig up the names of all the Pagan/metaphysical/new age shops in our area and those within a four hour drive. We make laminated color copies of our flyer for them. (It looks very nice.) Then we draft a cover letter, put all of that in a mailing tube and send them out. Almost every shop that we have ever mailed to was cooperative and posted our (very attractive) poster in a prominent area of their shop. It costs a bit of money to do this, but it pays off. For PUF VII, we had two groups of people from Chicago. That is quite a distance to travel for a Pagan festival, but they thought it looked so good, they just had to come.

Speaking of the Chicago connection, this falls under the heading of "You just never know whom your advertising will reach." I got a phone call from a local Pagan who had just heard of PUF and was very excited about it. She wanted to make reservations right away. I was only too happy to take her money, and I asked her how she had heard of us. Seems she got a call from a friend of hers who lived in the aforementioned Chicago who had seen a poster in her local Pagan shop. So, our advertising in Illinois got us three reservations from Tennessee. Go figure.

Staff & guests behind the PUF sheep signs

Pre-registration
Don't guess who's coming to dinner.

No matter if your festival is large or small, daytrip only or a week long, getting reservations paid in advance will be a great help to you. There are a couple of reasons for using this idea. One, this will give you money early, and you will have plenty in hand to cover expenses instead of taking it out of your pocket up front. The site, food, toilet paper, travel expenses for the VIPs and everything else has to be bought and paid for in advance. With pre-registration, you will have the money to take care of all that. And, you will have a real good idea of how many will be attending your festival, so you can plan accordingly.

What if you don't get folks to pre-register? That means you have to use guesswork or a crystal ball. You figure your needs based on how many folks have shown an interest in attending. Say you figure that about 150 folks will be attending. You buy food for 150 and make all the other arrangements based on that number. Come the day of the festival seventy-five folks show up. You are out a lot of money, my friend. What if, on the day of the festival, 275 folks show up, and you only have camping facilities and food for 150? You are in just as much trouble, and people are going to be irate. Say it with me, RESERVATIONS ARE GOOD.

In many ways getting folks to pre-register is a big PAIN IN THE ASS. You have to remind people constantly, send them emails and postcards and show up at other local events to tell them about your festival. If you want anyone to show up for your festival, you have to do all of those things anyway. Why not add to all that effort, getting their money up front?

First, figure out how many people you can comfortably accommodate at your site. Be realistic here; not everyone is friendly enough to sleep cheek to jowl with everyone else. So how many can attend? If it is a camping only event, you still must have enough room for tents and all the other activities of the weekend. For a camping only event, the bookkeeping is a little easier. You only have to keep count of the people who pre-register and keep an eye on the total number allowed.

If your event site has cabins, you have yet another problem. If you are selling cabin space or beds, you have to keep track of how many beds you have filled so that you don't sell the same bed twice. Selling beds will make you crazy, I guarantee. But there are ways to do it. The first year we sold beds, we kept a running list in a notebook (not computer literate, remember). We had the total number of beds, and just made a list of everyone who wanted space with names and addresses and how much they paid. There was much confusion, but we managed not to sell the same bed twice. That was a miracle. We had people download the admission form and mail that and a check to us. It worked pretty well, but I worried constantly that we had oversold the beds or that we had put two parties in the same cabin.

    The second year, we figured out a way to take the reservations and keep the sleeping arrangements straight and not go nuts. It was so simple; I pounded my head on the wall because I did not think of it before. (That happens a lot.) The park provided a map of the site with all the cabins and other buildings drawn in. We made a big copy of the map, put it on foam core and then wrote the people's names next to the cabins, which we numbered as we sold them. We wrote it in erasable ink, so that we could change things around if necessary. That made everything so much easier.

    My suggestion to you is that if you are selling beds, make a map. Hang it somewhere that will not be disturbed, and add the names to it on a daily basis. Even if you are not selling beds, make a map anyway and draw in everything. It will give you a quick answer as to where to place something new.

    How do you get them to send in their money early? After all, we all know that we Pagans are notorious for waiting till the last minute. Answer: simply give them a price break if they reserve early. When the tickets go on sale, there is a starting price for the first month. This price increases every month after that. The "at the door" price locks in two weeks before the festival. If you make the savings substantial enough, folks will rush to buy tickets. And you will breathe much easier.

    We have added a PayPal button to our website for payment. It too is a great tool for getting the pre-registration money because it makes it easy to pay. No one has to make out a check and go to the post office and mail it. They can pay instantly. A person simply checks to see how much they need to pay according to how many folks and how many beds, etc., and hits the PayPal button. They are taken to the PayPal site where they pay their money and get a confirmation. We check the PayPal website everyday to see who has paid and how much they paid, and we add them to the list along with how many beds they need and how many days they will be staying. Folks that are tent camping also use this system. It has made the job of keeping the money, the people and the sleeping arrangements so much easier. Use it! You will not be sorry. This alone will not stop all the confusion; you will still have people contact you to see if you have received their money. Ask them if they have received a confirmation from PayPal, and assure them that means you have their reservation. You may have to go the extra step of looking it up for confirmation, but do it—everyone will be happier. To save the confusion, you may want to just mail a confirmation postcard or send an email to everyone who pays by PayPal.

There is another benefit to using PayPal. You can get a debit card for your account. You can use this to pay for everything connected to the festival. You will get a monthly readout of what you spend and where. It makes the bookkeeping so easy.

Pre-registration also means that you need to get started even earlier, which only means that the madness of the festival starts sooner. You have to get your website up and flyers ready several months in advance. The advantage this gives you is that folks will see the information earlier, and it will give them a chance to make plans to come.

Your staff members that keep track of all things relating to reservations, will need to have frequent meetings to keep everything straight. Otherwise, who paid what and who sleeps where will become a logistical nightmare very quickly. You will really have to get organized and stay on top of it. Having frequent meetings will help bring everyone up to speed. It is also nice to have someone with whom to bemoan your confused state. We have found that drinking copious amounts of alcohol seems to help quite a bit.

We have, over the years, offered a group discount. Unfortunately, at first we were not specific enough about it. We simply said that if you had a group of eight or more, you got a ten percent discount off the total price. We did not tell folks that they needed to make all the reservations at the same time and send the money in all at once. Consequently, we had money dribbling in over several weeks from different people in the same group. Some of those people who paid late had to sleep on the floor. Not only was the math so painful, but also the groups expected us to hold beds for all of their members, even the ones who had not paid yet. I wanted to pull my hair out by the roots.

Now, we still offer a group discount for numbers over eight, and we offer a family discount with a money cap. Sometimes those two things overlap. We ask that anyone entitled to discounts email us and give us all the facts, then we figure out which fee is the cheapest and email them back with that amount. It takes a bit of time to do all this, but everyone feels that they are getting a good deal, and they are happy campers. (Sorry couldn't help myself.) They come to the festival happy, and everyone's mood is pretty positive.

We also have a "no refund" policy that kicks in thirty days before the festival. It is stated on the website very plainly. There is a very good reason for this; by the time you are thirty days from the festival date, you have already bought most of the dry foods, paper products, batteries, soap, etc., based on your total. That money is spent; you don't have it anymore. How can you refund it? That is not to say we have never refunded after the thirty-day limit; we have. Sometimes emergencies happen, hospital visits happen and family emergencies also happen, and we try to be reasonable. A broken leg is an emergency that will stop a person from coming to a festival in the woods. A crummy, rainy weekend is not. That will be your call, and you will possibly make some enemies, but there is no way around it. You must do what is best for the health of your festival. Try and be reasonable, and don't lose your temper; it is bad for your blood pressure.

There are a million details about your festival that will make you crazy, trip you up and make you want to retire to a cave somewhere in the mountains. Getting people to pre-register will help you from going completely around the bend. Maybe.

⳽The Kid Thing⳾
It takes a village and then some.

How well this has worked over the years has ebbed and flowed. Some years it has been really wonderful, and some years it has been a total nightmare. But we keep trying to fine-tune it because we feel that it is important.

The first year, we decided to have classes for the children. This is something that many festivals do not offer, but we did not know that at the time. The thinking was that kid's classes would free up the parents to go to workshops, and it would be fun for the kids. A wonderful woman, Blue Rain, planned the children's activities. She is a certified daycare person and very knowledgeable, and she is great with the kids. We are very lucky to have her. She did most of the work, but we all helped a little. Basically, she planned activities that would keep the kids busy, that weren't too difficult, and the items needed would be cheap. We worried about having kids in our care and spent a lot of time discussing what could go wrong. As it turned out, lots of things can go wrong when dealing with kids. They can get hurt; they can get sick; a non-custodial parent could try and pick them up from us, and we would be none the wiser; we might accidentally feed them something to which they were allergic—it is a long and scary list. We decided that parents would sign the kids in and out of care and write down who was allowed to collect them as well. We also added food and other allergies on the information sheet. Children would have a paper tag to wear around their necks that had all the information written on it. We would not medicate or change diapers; one must draw the line somewhere. We thought that would take care of any problems that might arise. Alas, we were so naive.

The children's activities went pretty well the first year. We intended for the parents to help out so that Blue Rain would not be overwhelmed with kids, and some parents did step up to the plate. But not everyone participated; some just dropped off their kids and ran away. We had devised no way to keep track of who helped out and who did not nor did we set up a schedule. By the end of the day, we decided that we had to be more organized in how we handled the parental helpers. The paper badges for the kids did not work so well; they just lost them or tore them off or ate them. Thankfully, there were not too many children, and we managed to keep track of them all. But we knew that we had to rethink our methods in the kid area.

When we moved to our new site, we decided to use one of the cabins without bunks for the children's activities. It was very large, completely empty and had a big closet for storage. It was perfect for our needs. There was only one little problem; it had no door. We used a baby gate over the doorway to keep the children corralled. We really put our heads together on the children's activities. We felt that we would have a lot more children, and we wanted everything to go smoothly. We required the parents to help out. They would sign their children in and then pick a block of time to work their volunteer shift. That would relieve the burden on Blue Rain. She slaved over the activities and bought lots of clay, crayons, chalk and snacks for the kids. "Bring the ankle biters on," we cried, because we were ready. We thought.

We still had problems getting parents to help out, getting them to fill out paperwork and getting staff members to work in the kid's area. We had trouble keeping the kids happy; the older ones did not like being trapped in with the little kids. Many of the volunteers allowed the children to run amok…that is not quite correct. Some of the volunteers did not have a firm hand with the children, and the children ran amok all by themselves. I have seen volunteers returning from a 1.5-hour stint with the children who looked like they had been dragged backwards through a knothole by a mad dog. One man approached me after his wife had done her time with the kids to thank me for allowing her to have that experience. He claimed that her biological clock had frozen during her work shift with the children, and now she would not be annoying him about having children of their own. It is good to make people happy.

On the other hand, we had folks that were childless who wanted to play and spent hours happily conducting activities and telling stories to the kids. They took them outside to play ball, to play Frisbee, to hike and to mud paint. One year we had a treasure hunt in the sand at the volleyball court for geodes. Of course that was the year that we forgot the hammer to break the geodes. Good thing we are inventive.

We have tried lots of ways to deal with the children over the years.

We have tried having no childcare, and that was a disaster. We have tried asking parents to pay $10 extra for childcare; with this money we intended to hire outside caregivers and give our long-suffering staff a break. We had no takers. We have placed a staff member in with the kids and given them some volunteers as back up. The children ate the timid for lunch. We have had years when we tried to be laid back and relax the rules a bit; folks sent their kids to the children's area and did not come themselves. There have been years that we had roving gangs of kids wreaking havoc all over the site. All in all, it seems that every year we have something that goes terribly wrong. But we keep trying to fine-tune the system. And at least—as of this writing—none of the children have been eaten by bears.

We have thought long and hard about childcare, and maybe we have hit upon the right combination. We have activities for the children, and the children are broken up into age groups. We set up the area for the 3 to 7's with a table or two along each wall. There is a coloring area with coloring books, coloring sheets, plain paper, crayons, chalk and pencils. There is sculpting with clay, play dough and items the children can use to create great works of art. There is an area with all sorts of items that may be glued onto paper; this is our imagination corner. We have a painting corner with water paints, finger paints and brushes. There is also a corner for storytelling. The children pick the activities in which they want to participate, and that makes them happy. Even three-year-olds can color. We also take them outside to just run and play. This age group also does a mud painting outside. We ask the parents to send a large T-shirt to keep their clothes clean and a blanket or a mat in case their child wants to take a nap.

The 7 to 11's are set up in the front yard of the children's building. They have actual workshops. This gets a little more complicated and work intensive. We have picked craft workshops that are not too difficult for the kids to do and not too difficult to teach. Over the years there has been a candle-making class, a mask-making class and everyone's favorite, mud painting. For ideas on crafts and outside activities, go to your favorite bookstore and get a copy of Circle Round. That is a great one for Pagan kids. You can also find other books with good ideas, not just for Pagan kids. Go to craft stores and see what they have to offer; that is where you will find the ingredients for mud painting. There is a great wholesale catalogue called

Oriental Trading that has lots of craft kits for multiple kids. It even breaks down the cost per child in each kit. That is important; you need to keep it cheap. There is a tendency to get excited over the crafts for the kids and spend too much money. Or is that just me?

If you think back on your own camping days, you will remember the things you did that were fun: treasure hunts, nature walks where you discover cool items, macaroni-covered boxes spray-painted gold. To these kids, those will be new ideas. Go for it!

You must buy enough craft stuff to accommodate all the kids at the festival, so no one is left out. To figure how many coffee cans you need to make drums, take your pre-registration head count of kids and add ten percent. That should be a close figure. If you under guess, you can always find a discount store, so don't panic.

Plan extra indoor activities—more than you will need. This is in case it rains, and you can't do the outdoor activities. We have tried to build a solar oven to bake cookies for the past three years, and it always rains us out. We have a staff member who brings a TV/DVD player. This has saved many a rainy day.

Tell the parents that they must escort their child to childcare for the first session. At that time, they fill out paperwork on the child and sign up for 1.5 hours of volunteer work. There will be some who grumble, but most of the parents will do their part. In past years we have had parents that just did not want to be involved in the care of kids. So we cut deals with them; some do extra shifts of work to make up the difference, and from some we take monetary bribes.

We have tried over the years to have something for the teens too. Kids over the age of 12 can go to class with a parent if they wish to do so. They just have to behave. We have an area set up for the teens that is just for them. There are games, cards, music and snacks. We encourage teenagers to bring cards and games that they are into to the festival. There are no organized classes for them; it is very free form, and they can design the kind of things they want to do. We have a hot dog roast at the lake every evening of the festival, and of course, they are welcome at the drumming circle. We do ask that a parent accompany children under the age of 16 to the adult bonfire.

We also have a set of guidelines. This information is sent out to anyone who registers and includes children in their party. This way there are no surprises for them; they know exactly what is offered and what is expected of them in return. It may seem a bit anal-retentive (Damn, I use that word a lot!). Over the years, I have learned that you have to be upfront about how things work with the festival. People have a tendency to push the envelope; we just let them know where the flaps are.

Here are the guidelines that we send out to folks who register with children. It is also in our program.

Children Info

PUF is a family-oriented event. We welcome your children here. We want them to be safe at all times, and we want them to have a good time. We hope that this event will be something they remember fondly and look forward to attending each year. With that in mind, we have certain standards in place.

- We require that a parent or guardian accompany children under the age of three at all times.
- Children between the ages of 3 and 7 may participate in activities in our Kid's Area. In this area, we have separate stations set up for coloring, clay, finger painting and arts and crafts. The children are encouraged to find the activities that interest them. Adults guide the younger ones. All these activities are geared for children within this age group. We also have play periods outside. We do not change diapers; so all children must be potty trained.
- Children age 7 through 11 have actual workshops that will interest them. These include making candles, kites, musical instruments and masks. We also have hikes and other outdoor activities. The workshops for the children last 1.5 hours each and run at the same time as the adult workshops. There is a workshop for each time period. The full list will be posted on the website but may also be obtained by mail.

- The Children's Activities Coordinator is a member of our volunteer staff. Please instruct your child to be polite and cooperative.
- You must sign your child into and out of our care. There will be paperwork to fill out pertaining to your child's needs. Do not simply send your child to the activities building. The Security Thugs will hunt you down.
- You will be asked who else can collect your child from our care when you fill out the paperwork. Do not send anyone whose name is not on the list to collect your child as they will not be released.
- Children's activities run on the adult class schedule. There is a break for lunch; please collect your child at that time.
- Please collect your child promptly at the end of the day.
- Failure to collect your child at the appointed times may result in loss of children's activities privileges.
- You must volunteer 1.5 hours in the children's activities area for each child that you bring.
- You must sign up for volunteer time when you bring your child and sign him/her into care.
- Explain to your child that they MUST remain in care until you come for them.
- We do not administer medicine; please give your child his/her medication before you bring them to care. If your child needs a dose of medicine while in our care, please come and administer it to your child at the proper time.
- Please bring a large T-shirt for your child to wear for messy activities.
- If your child is young, please bring a pillow and blanket, so they may nap if they wish.
- All children under the age of 11 must be in the care or in the company of a parent or guardian. If any children are found wandering, they will be sold to the highest bidder.
- Children over the age of 11 may attend classes with a parent. They are expected to behave as adults.

- If you send your child to children's activities with a walkie-talkie, please know that the item will be turned off and placed in a closet, only to be used if your child has an emergency.
- There is a special gathering place for teens and activities for them. Your teens are encouraged to bring games and cards that they would like to share with others. They may also attend classes if they desire.
- There will be a hot dog roast each evening of the festival; we encourage your teen to attend. They are also welcome at the adult bonfire, drumming circle and the Guedra. If they are under the age of 16, they must be in the company of a parent.
- Failure to adhere to these guidelines will result in your child not being allowed to participate in children's activities.

**THANK YOU FOR YOUR COOPERATION
WITH OUR STAFF**

Despite your best efforts to accommodate kids, you will find people who leave their kids in the cabin or tent while they go play, kids who are running loose with no adult watching over them and parents who hand their kid over to anyone who will watch them and then disappear for hours. To me, these things are not acceptable. I understand the need for parents to cut loose and have some down time. I raised three kids, I really understand. But, you must make parents understand that their children are their responsibility. It may well take a village to raise a child, but that does not mean that parents can abdicate their responsibility.

Whatever you decide to do, whichever system or lack of system you pick, have fun with it, and the kids will have fun too. If you have members of your staff that do not like children, don't send them to help out with the kids. It will be a disaster. On the other hand, don't stick your child-loving staff members with the kids the entire weekend; they will suffer burn out. Make sure they get breaks, and remember that they will probably need large doses of alcohol afterward. Childcare is a sticky issue; just keep playing with it, and eventually you will hit on what works the best for you. Good luck!

Fun with jumbo bubbles

ॐWorkshops/Classesॐ
Here be dragons.

I think that workshops are the heart of any festival. This is the main reason that people come to festivals; at least that is what I think. They want to learn. Sure, they come to play in the woods, see old friends, dance and attend ritual. They want to be entertained, but they want to be educated as well. Your job is to have the best workshops that you can muster. So where do you start? The same place as before. Look at all the people you know and see if any of them are interested in teaching a class on a subject in which they are well versed.

The first year of our festival, I went through my own folks looking for anyone who had an area of expertise and who wanted to share their knowledge with others. When I had exhausted that source, I went to some of the local covens and asked for help. I asked them for some volunteers to facilitate classes. I knew that just like us, many of the covens had some folks whom they considered experts in various fields. Several people stepped up to the plate and volunteered to teach. We only had about a half dozen classes the first year, and I ended up teaching several of them. Some people that I expected to teach were kind of shy about going outside of their own group. On the other hand, some people who I never expected to teach were the first ones to agree. You just don't know how people will respond.

We were fairly primitive the first couple of years and had classes under the trees. It was very cool to see Pagans sitting under trees and having classes. I enjoyed walking from class to class, listening and watching the level of participation. People really enjoyed the opportunity to sit down and learn from others. They were not shy with questions either, and I took that as a good sign. I was surprised to see that classes were full! One thing I discovered, to my amazement, was that most of the people who attended were new to Paganism and were solitary practitioners. This was a wonderful opportunity for them to learn from others who had practiced for a long time. Most attendees had only learned from books, and they took to this chance for hands-on learning like ducks to water. They were excited, and no wonder; here were real live folks to ask questions of and get answers from. I watched their horizons open up with the experience of hanging out with like-minded folks. It was a beautiful thing. Intellectually, I knew that classes were important to a festival, but it was not until that moment when I saw the light in the eyes of the students that I really understood how important they were. I was, and still am, very proud of that moment.

The second year, we had more classes to offer. People began to lose their shyness and wanted to share their knowledge. I knew that I wanted more classes, or more subjects; people were hungry for knowledge, and I wanted to feed them. We took all comers too because we wanted to fill up the space with classes. We still had the classes under the trees, and again there was wonderful participation.

By the third year, we were beginning to look like a real festival, and lots of people were suddenly interested in doing workshops for us—so many in fact that we had to make a list of classes that people were offering to present. I got my wish for more classes. We went through the list and picked and chose the ones we wanted. The idea being that we did not want all the classes to be a Wicca 101. The variety we ended up with was excellent, and before we knew it, we had over twenty workshops scheduled. Wow!

After looking over that list, I decided that I wanted someone with a different spin on Paganism. All the class facilitators were locals, and while they were offering good classes, I wanted something more. So, this was where my meeting Tony Kail paid off. He agreed to come and present a workshop for us, but I think that he really came out just for the opportunity to observe real live Pagans in their native habitat. So we had a real headliner, and we were thrilled beyond words.

Once we went over the list of classes and decided on which classes to hold, we had to create a schedule. There are only so many hours in the day (unless I want to move to Jupiter), and we had to plan around meals. We finally, after much angst, set up a working schedule and plugged the classes into it. It gave us two class periods before lunch and three more after lunch. Each class block was 1.5 hours with a ten-minute break in between classes. I figured that was enough time to hit the bathroom and grab a cigarette in between workshops. It also provided a thirty-minute lunch period. It was rearranged several times before we were happy with it, and even then I was not terribly thrilled with the end results. The workshops ran late into the day so that supper and ritual was pushed back much later that I wanted. We also had to run classes up against each other, but we had room for our headliners to be in a class block without competition. So I finally quit tweaking it and left it alone.

Then we had to decide where to hold the classes. The new site had a main hall with lots of tables and benches for meals, but it could also pull double duty as classroom space. It is a really big hall. We could put our headliners and the classes we thought would have the largest draw there. But, it needed to be empty during the last class time of the day so that we could set it up for dinner. Not a problem. We arranged classes accordingly and left it empty for the last class block of the day. We also decided to use the pavilion for workshops and the big tree next to the ritual field too. That gave us three separate places to hold workshops. So we still had Pagans under the trees.

Everyone who attended Tony Kail's class was very impressed with his presentation. He did a bang-up workshop. He is so incredibly knowledgeable about all types of religious practices, and he brought lots of show and tell stuff. He laid out pictures, books and artifacts that included every religious practice from Vodoun to Wicca. He even brought a slide show. We did not have a screen for him (too poor), so we hung up a sheet. Primitive, but effective. He was great! So our first real headliner was a local non-Pagan, and everyone loved him.

That year, we invited Grey Cat as well, and the people who attended her "Ritual Etiquette for Beginners" class were very impressed. Many of them commented that they felt much more relaxed about attending ritual with a large group. She did a great job telling them what to expect and how to behave. Everyone was very good in ritual.

The fourth year of the festival, people began to contact us in droves to offer classes. We found that almost too many people wanted to come and play with us. At this point in the proceedings, a fellow named M. R. Sellars, who is an author, contacted me. He wrote (and still does) murder mysteries with a Pagan twist. His protagonist is a Witch who in daily life is a computer jockey but in his spare time investigates occult crime. Mr. Sellars was looking for festivals that might be interested in having him do workshops. I certainly was interested, especially after I looked at his website. So, we made a deal; he would do two workshops and sell his books. A real live honest-to-goodness writer-type guy was coming to PUF! I was beside myself with joy.

To date we have had Tony Kail, Grey Cat, M. R. Sellars, Dorothy Morrison, Trish Telesco, Isaac Bonewits, Swain Wodening, Anne Moura, Ashleen O'Gaia and CanyonDancer, Josephine Dunn and Colston Brown as our guests. I consider us lucky and privileged to have been host to these folks.

As you grow, you will find that more and more people want to participate. Your job is to make sure that the teachers really have something to offer, and there is a great variety. The bigger your festival gets the less you will have to worry about variety, but you will still have to worry about quality.

We ask all of our workshop facilitators to give us a bio—who they are, what their training is, where they have taught before. We also ask for an outline of the class they will be teaching. We ask each teacher to prepare two workshops for us, one to present and one in reserve in case we lose a class. Once you have a year where you lose teachers the week of festival because of divorce, car accidents and chicken pox, you too will adopt this policy. We pick the class that we like the best from the two they submit. Then we contact them and let them know which class we picked and ask for commitment from them. We pick classes with different themes and attempt to keep balance in the workshops. We try not to have fourteen classes on meditation or the like.

Then we plug the classes in the existing schedule. It might not seem hard, but it drives me crazy. We have so many classes now that there are usually three or four in the same class block. People have to pick what they want to see. I want very different classes in each class block. It is my belief (however deluded) that most people are looking for the same thing, a specific belief system or making tools or learning about as many different paths as possible and so on. Therefore, I do not put all of my craft classes in the same block, and I spread out my Celtic, Roman and Strega, etc., workshops throughout the day as well. Then I plug in all the other classes around them. I also never put my Big-Nose Witches up against each other because everyone wants to see him or her. At this point when the schedule is

Workshops/Classes 53

complete, we contact the presenters and tell them when their class is scheduled. We usually have to rearrange a bit to accommodate everyone because of travel plans and work schedules and what not. I promise you that I lose sleep over the class schedule. But then, I am kinda nuts.

When you are holding a local festival, you want to work hard to keep everyone's good will. So you talk to everyone who offers to teach a class, and you try hard not to leave anyone out. It can be really sticky, like walking on a sword's edge. (Sorry about the mixed metaphor.) Anyway, you want good classes, so you must pick people who really know their stuff. Yet, you don't want to insult anyone either. It is a tough job. When your festival is small, you know everyone who wants to teach, and you are familiar with each person's skills, or you know someone who is and you can ask them.

When your festival gets bigger, this becomes a bigger problem. People from all over apply to teach, and sometimes you don't know them. So you ask around and see if anyone you trust knows them. Truly, sometimes people just come out of the woodwork, and you can't find a soul to give you feedback. In that case, you just go with your gut. Of course I am not saying this always works. We have had a few duds over the years. We just weed them out and keep going. On the other hand, we have also had some great presenters who we did not know before the festival. I find that I pray a lot in the run-up to PUF.

We have two ways of keeping the quality up with the workshops. First, our Workshop Coordinator ghosts around to all of the classes and spends some time observing. Second are the comment cards. We decided that we wanted feedback from the attendees, not just our own observations. So we hand out comment cards at the beginning of each class. We really read them. Some of them are really funny, like the ones that tell us how evil M. R. Sellars really is—as if we didn't know. For the most part, the comments are very positive, and some are really amusing. The comment cards also tell us if a presenter was not organized, not a good teacher or was just full of bull. And this is where you separate the sheep from the goats, my dears. We use these cards to decide who comes back and who doesn't. If a lot of the comments are negative about a class or a facilitator, we mark them off for the next year. It is tough love.

Many times, when dealing with presenters, you are going to find a great big ego in a human suit—people who are just full of themselves and people who are HIGH maintenance. You have to decide if the information they present and the people they draw to your festival are worth the hassle to you. Sometimes they are, and you ask them back. Sometimes they are not and you don't. Over the years I have been amazed at the Big-Nose Witches who were so down to earth and easy to accommodate and the folks who only thought they were Big-Nose Witches who were such a pain.

People are contacting us earlier each year to ask to facilitate a workshop. That is a mixed blessing. At this point, our class schedule fills up early, and some of the folks who have presented workshops in years past get bumped. We hate that, but we tell them to get with us sooner next time. At this point, I fear we may be forced to schedule classes at PUF for the next PUF.

Don't be afraid to pick classes that are outside of what you think of as "Pagan." We have had workshops on Hindu mantras, Buddhist prayers and yoga. Folks loved them. Most of our classes are admittedly basic. That is because many of the people who attend are new to the Craft. And too, I am a little wary of having an advanced class on a subject that takes years to study. We have, over the years, added more advanced classes on subjects that we have taught before. This, I hope, gives us something for everyone.

Picking teachers and classes is something that you have to handle with kid gloves. You want to keep everyone happy, if possible. You want good classes. You don't want to piss off too many folks. Plus you want to avoid making yourself nuts. The only way to learn this process is on-the-job training.

⊰Merchants⊱
Cool things to buy!

I should probably start this section with a disclaimer because I know that I am going to piss off some folks. It won't be the first time nor will it be the last. But I think that I can talk frankly about merchants here because I am one. Merchants can be a royal pain to deal with under the best of circumstances. They are coming to the event to make money and make contacts. This is their livelihood. They are not coming to play or to attend classes. It is business. Given that, they want to be in a position to make the most amount of money possible. They don't want to be down in a hole someplace where no one can find them. They don't want to be strung out all over the place because people might give up and not visit all the merchants. They don't want to be separated from each other. They will arrive early and leave late, if you let them. They will try to set up where they want to set up. They will tell you how you need to run your event. They will yell the loudest if there is something to yell about. Remember that it is not personal, it is just business.

Your job, if you are the person in charge of merchants, is to be as accommodating as you can be without screwing yourself up. You must be firm. And you must remember that this is a two-way relationship; without them your event will not be so entertaining, and without you they have no place to sell their wares. The festival needs them, and honey, they need the festival. Try and establish a "You wash my back and I'll wash your back" relationship with your merchants.

We want a large variety of vendors at PUF, not one or two Pagan superstores. So we ask for a list of items from each vendor. We eliminate the duplicates, or sometimes we ask a vendor not to display a certain item because we already have a vendor who carries that item. We ask each vendor to sign a contract with the festival before we approve him or her to vend. This has done three things for us. We have a wide range of merchandise, much of which is hand-made. We have very loyal merchants who come back year after year because we protect their interests. Last but not least, it has really annoyed a number of merchants who will not come to

PUF because we are too anal. Oh, well.

The journey from having no merchants to being able to pick and choose the best merchants was a long one. The first year, the idea of merchants never crossed my mind. The second year, thanks to our advertising on the net, some Pagan merchants heard about us and wanted to come and play too. We had to find a good place for them with plenty of shade. We hunted around the site and finally found the perfect place to put them—under a long line of trees close to the pavilion that we were using for all the main activities. I was so excited to have merchants that I did not care what they sold that year.

The next year of the festival, we had more merchants. Word had gotten out. Many of them arrived before the staff had gotten on site. That was not cool. They began to set up wherever they wanted since no one was there to tell them otherwise; they just did it.

The merchants wanted to set up close to the main hall since that is where most of the people are. Many of the merchants wanted to camp with their merchandise. I don't blame them; I would feel the same way. But the layout (or lack of one) made that almost impossible. I say almost. Camping happened, but it was not comfortable. Merchandise tents and camping tents were all together in a space that was too small by far to hold them. It gave me a headache. The merchants were in the way of classes and meals. Still, the shoppers did not complain; they all looked as happy as hogs in slop. The merchants did not complain because they made money. But I must tell you it was a regular goat screw.

The following year I got to the site early (the night before) and was ready for the merchants when they arrived. We set them up close to the hall but farther away than the year before. It was a better set-up, but it was still a traffic jam. The merchant tents were in a line, kind of, but it looked more like a line laid out by a drunken snake than anything else. There still was no real order. Several of the merchants wanted electricity; this was one of those things that I had not considered in advance. But we tried to accommodate by running outdoor extension cords from the main hall to the booths. Great idea, huh? When the merchants fired up lights and power tools, it blew the circuits in the main hall. That was fun.

The next year, we put the merchants on the far end of the field from the main hall. I had two reasons for doing this; they could drive right on to the field and not have to haul their merchandise too far, it moved the merchants away from the main hall and gave them lots of room to set up merchant tents and sleeping tents. We rented a port-a-potty for the merchant area. I thought it was a great setup. Everyone bitched about how far a walk it was to the merchant area.

After several nervous breakdowns, I thought we had the merchants in a happy place. We put them close to the main hall but behind and to the side of it, so they did not interfere with traffic. They were close to the main hall, the ritual field and most of the action. But not too close. We set up the meet-point of the camp in their area. This brought people to see what was happening, and they hung out. And the merchants didn't feel like the festival was happening and they were not getting to play. Sounds great, right? It was, until the storm of the century blew through the camp and created a river that ran right through the merchant area. What a mess that was. We survived and muddled through. We spread straw to try and create a place to walk that was not ankle deep in mud. I guess we will just keep moving merchant row until we find the perfect place for it.

We have a staff member in charge of taking care of the merchants. This is the person who makes arrangements with the folks who want to vend at PUF, who helps any merchant who needs it and gives a vendor a warm trustworthy body to mind their booth while they take a potty break. So many merchants travel alone that this has really helped them out. He is also the person who accepts or rejects vendors and the person that gets yelled at by those who are turned down.

We try to give our merchants a few perks. For example, they get in the dinner line first so that they can eat and get back to work. We have rigged up lights for the merchant area, so folks can shop at night. And occasionally we have even had a Midnight Madness Sale in vendor row. That is fun. Unfortunately, no one gets individual electricity in their booth anymore. Hey, you can't have it all!

Last but not least, love your merchants. Pat them on the head and tell them how happy you are to have them with you. They work hard for the money.

ෂMapsක
Directions! What a concept!

First, you need a map to get to your location. If you have a website, great! Add a link to a good map/direction website or to the site you are using if they have one. But a word to the wise—check the directions on that link. Once we took directions straight off the website of the park we were using, and they were wrong. Check your facts, and if they are incorrect, write your own. If you are making flyers and don't have a website, then add very good directions.

Remember to write the directions so that people coming from the north, south, east or west can find the place. Don't just write the directions from your town. You will have folks wandering around in the dark. You will anyway, no matter what you do, but maybe this way you will have less of them.

Drive out to your site and really look at the lay of the land as you go. Find out if there are any ordinances against posting signs and work around that. Decide where to put signs for people to follow. Signs complete with arrows pointing the way are a bonus. We put signs at the interstate exit, the bottom of the ramp and at every turn to the site. We put a couple of more inside the park. No matter how well you think that you have posted the way, some folks will get lost. So add a few more signs than you think you need.

Remember that many people will be coming to a place they have never been before, and they will need to be guided into the site. Many of them will be arriving in the dark as well, so make those signs highly visible. Just because you have a good sense of direction, remember that not everyone does.

We have had signs printed; they are plastic with BIG red letters and arrows to point the way. They were not cheap—about $25 per sign. But they have lasted us for three years and counting, so I consider them a good investment. We have only had one sign stolen so far. Our signs only say, "PUF." They do not say, "BIG BUNCH OF PAGANS PLAYING IN THE WOODS!" That tends to keep down the number of folks who show up with torches and pitchforks. People who know what they are looking for will see the signs, and all the rest of the folks who see them will just wonder what the hell PUF is. Every year as we put them up and take them down, I swear if anyone asks me what PUF stands for I will say, "Presbyterians United in Faith." While we are on this subject, remember to send someone out occasionally during the weekend to check and make sure that all your signs are still in place. For some reason, there are people who think that moving directional signs or stealing them is really amusing.

Do what you can to really secure the signs to whatever tree or post you put them on. One year, one of the signs was not secured very well, the wind blew, and the sign turned upside-down with the arrow pointing the wrong direction. That might sound amusing, but when several folks actually went the wrong way and got lost, well you get the picture.

Despite all the precautions we use to get folks safely to site, every year we have lost people. We post a cell phone number on our flyers and website to help our lost sheep find their way. One year we had folks drive in from Chicago, and they were lost somewhere in Clarksville, Tennessee. Trust me, that is quite a way from the park we use. They called us, and we were able to guide them in to site. We even waited up for them to arrive. When they finally made it in, they were really glad to see us. No wonder, being a bunch of Yankee Pagans lost in the boondocks of the Bible-banging South is pretty scary. The cell phone has helped several of our folks find us and has been a real boon.

We have a map of the camp as well, and that is in the program that we hand out. This helps people get acclimated to the site and figure out where everything is and how to get there. It has all the cabins numbered, the main hall, classroom space, merchant row, tent camping and bathhouses. People really use it. With that map, the only excuse they have for wandering around lost is because they want to be lost.

Even if you do not have cabins, I still recommend a map of the site. It will keep tempers from becoming frayed because folks can't find the bathhouse or whatever. You can add warnings about muddy places to stay away from or dragons or any other hazards on your site. It will also keep you from having to stop what you are doing in order to give directions forty-two times a day. It is worth the effort.

ঞRitualॐ
Seating for 200, please.

Ah, ritual. I love ritual. We have had some great ones over the years. Some of them were profound, some were funny, and some were just very interesting. The first year I, by default, knew I was going to run the ritual. From that point on it became an experiment in terror. I myself had never run a ritual for 100 people. I think the most folks that I ever had in ritual were about forty. Since I was pretty ignorant, I did quite a bit of studying before the festival, so I could know what to expect. After all, running a ritual for 100 people in a very public venue is vastly different from running a ritual for thirty people in your back yard.

I wanted the ritual and festival to be an example of cooperation between different groups and different trads. With that in mind I asked the leaders of Oak, Ash and Thorn if they would be willing to join with my group so that we could do the ritual together. They agreed and we planned a very simple, traditional Wiccan ritual.

We planned on eating the evening meal after ritual. I personally find that it is sometimes hard to raise energy on a full stomach. Plus, people get to eating and socializing, and it is hard to get them going in the direction of ritual. My group usually plans our events this way simply as a matter of preference. I must admit that I did not think about people who did it differently. Some of the other groups that participated did food first and then ritual, and that is how they wanted it done. Consequently, there was a lot of *discussion* about the arrangements throughout the day. So, I bent and broke the first rule of festival organizing (because I did not know there were rules). I let public opinion sway me away from what I knew was a good idea. I compromised, and we set the food out and let the folks who wanted to eat first do so, and then the rest of the crowd could eat later, after ritual. It seemed so simple. However, this was not something that worked out very well. The people who wanted to wait till after ritual to eat were annoyed at the delay for the "eat first" people. The food had to be covered, to keep bugs and whatnot out, before ritual could start. Remember that when dealing with a nature religion, some times nature shows up. That took some time, causing more grumbling from the people who had eaten and wanted to get started with ritual. The folks who ate after ritual were annoyed because they felt as though they were getting leftovers, so they were unhappy about that. After all was said and done, it was almost impossible to get anyone to help clean up the dinner mess. Lesson learned. Food first, clean up the mess, then have ritual.

Once we finally got to ritual, it went very well despite the fact that two very different groups were doing it. There were some logistics to work out, and while there were some glaring differences in style, I was very happy with the end results. It was a pretty standard generic Pagan ritual. You know, set the circle, call the quarters, chant, and raise a little energy; nothing too spectacular. But it was good, and folks really enjoyed it. I found out after the fact that many of the people who stood circle that night had either never stood ritual before or had never stood ritual with more than a handful of others. I was amazed.

The second year, we had learned the lesson—food first and then ritual. Hungry people in ritual are grumpy people. It is hard enough to raise energy with a huge group of people who have never worked together before, under the best of circumstances. Trying to do it with growling stomachs and whining children is all bad. So it was decided; dinner would be served first, and then we would have ritual. Pagans with full tummies may not be able to raise huge amounts of energy, but they are much happier and easier to work with by far. Of course, some people complained, but I stuck to my guns. Small wonder, since I had spent hours cleaning up after dinner the year before.

The ritual that year was interesting and funny. We again had labyrinths, and after dark we lit them up with tea lights. The effect was amazing! They were wonderful to walk through and really put you in the mood for ritual. They were set up so that you walked through them and then down a corridor of torches and into the ritual space. We got a little fancy and had people standing down that corridor whispering lines from chants as the crowd filed in. Theatrical, but a nice effect.

After everyone was in the ritual space, the HP (my husband) came striding down the corridor of torches. He was wearing a long black cloak, black robes and a silver antler circlet on his head. The visual was impressive. What added to that visual image was the sight of his two attendants who were also clad in black and carrying light sabers. I could hear the "Darth Vader" music playing in my head as they marched toward us. I was not the only one; snickers ran around the circle. It might have been irreverent, but it was funny!

Ritual went well, and we chanted our brains out and got everyone revved up. I never realized until then how difficult it was to get a bunch of people to do more than just politely chant but to really raise energy. We used simple chants and repeated them till everyone had the rhythm, and then we went to the next chant. I worked my way around the circle encouraging folks to chant. By the time ritual was over, I had no voice and was sweating like a field hand. But it worked pretty well, and most folks seemed to really enjoy ritual. I was exhausted.

The third year, we asked Lady Morgaine to run the ritual and be the HPS. It only seemed fair since we had highjacked her site and her dates as well. She planned and led a beautiful ritual with a little help from one of our guys standing as her HP. We had 150 to 175 people in circle that night, and the energy we raised was quite impressive. Man, my hair was standing on end!

I found out a very important thing that night. I liked it when someone else ran the evening ritual. It took so much pressure off me, and I could be just a participant and really enjoy it. I decided then and there that I would begin the search for a group to do the ritual the next year. I did not have to look too far to find a volunteer. I picked someone I knew and whom I knew would do a great job. Problem solved, and I did not give it another thought.

That is until about two weeks before the festival opened. I got an email from the woman that I had asked to conduct the main ritual. She was not pleased that we had scheduled the ritual for after the feast. I explained that the logistics for ritual first and feast after were very difficult. I explained that we had tried it that way, and it was not a pleasant experience. I told her that we had done the "food first then ritual" way for a couple of years, and that was what folks expected. She told me that her coven did ritual first and then food, and that was the way she wanted to do it. I admitted that I preferred it that way myself, but we had to please several hundred other people, and we had to compromise on things. We went back and forth on email for several days on the subject, and finally she informed me that she would not be running the ritual nor would she or any of her group be coming to the festival.

That derailed my train but good! Hell, I almost had an aneurysm. Two weeks out from the festival and no ritual for Saturday night! After I got finished with my anxiety attack, I started a fast search for someone to step into the breach. Not too long a search as it turned out. The folks from Oak, Ash and Thorn and Tangled Moon agreed to take care of the ritual for us. Tragedy averted. Ritual ended that year with a quite spectacular flaming sword to fire the cone. You gotta love pyrotechnics.

Since that time, I have expanded the rituals for our festival. We have one on Friday night and one on Saturday night, and we have a few in between. I have prevailed on my Big-Nose Witches to run the main ritual on Saturday night. That has been wonderful. Isaac Bonewits has given classes on ritual construction, and the people from his class have run the main ritual. That was pretty nice. We have had guests do specific Trad rituals, and people get to see how others do things. Every year more folks step up to the plate for ritual, and I find that I can completely relax. (Okay, who am I kidding, I can never relax, but ritual is one less thing for me to worry about.)

I suggest that you find other groups or a special guest to run your ritual or rituals. Even with the possibility of someone canceling out on you at the last minute, it will still be easier. Your job is to be the troubleshooter, the chief cook and bottle washer, the problem solver. Let someone else do ritual. That way you can quietly sit in the background and give thanks that you still have most of your mind left. Now, let me say that you need to know the people running the ritual. You need to know what kind of ritual they will be presenting. Get with them in advance of the festival to go over all of the fine points. That way there are no unpleasant surprises for you, be they dull or dangerous.

If you really want to try your hand at running the ritual, I will give you a few pointers:

- ❖ Everything takes longer in a big group. If you are passing the chalice or lighting candles or doing any kind of business, you have to plan that time out, and add multiples of everything. Having only one chalice to pass around to 100 people takes awhile, and the folks who are waiting for it to get around the entire circle get bored. The one thing you never want in a ritual is boredom. So use four chalices. If you are passing out candles, use four baskets to pass them out. You can easily find people to do those jobs for you.
- ❖ Don't have everyone in circle ask for a special blessing or thank the gods or whatever. It might take hours.
- ❖ If you want everyone to write a request for something that they need as part of the ritual, have them do that before ritual starts. And bring lots of paper and pens.
- ❖ Don't make the ritual too complicated. A spiral dance is fun if you only have thirty people; it is a broken leg waiting to happen if you have 150.
- ❖ Make sure that you have lots of people with leather lungs to do the chanting so that everyone can hear and keep up. There is nothing worse than a ritual where people keep asking each other, "What are they saying?"
- ❖ Keep the chants simple too. Yes, I know you can put the words on paper, but the sound of 150 people rattling paper is distracting. Besides, the light will not be good enough for them to actually read anything.

Doing ritual for large groups of people takes practice and a willingness to be flexible in how you execute it. Like everything else at a festival, you make notes on what doesn't work, and don't do it again. And you make notes on what works well, and pat yourself on the back for a job well done. I also suggest that you get someone to give a "Ritual 101" class that will explain the logistics of standing circle with a large group of folks. We have run this class for several years, and it has been very helpful. It keeps folks from doing stupid things during ritual (most of the time).

Whether you do ritual yourself or give that job to someone you trust, you might want to include this list of ritual etiquette in your program.

Ritual Etiquette

- Don't take open containers of drink, alcoholic or otherwise, to ritual.
- Don't light up a cigarette or cigar inside of sacred space. (This seems so simple really. But I actually saw someone light a cigarette from an altar candle. Incredible!)
- If you've been drinking alcohol to excess or have used drugs before ritual, you need to sit outside of circle.
- If you need to leave the circle once the ritual has started, you need to cut a door. If you do not know how or don't feel comfortable doing it yourself, please ask someone to do it for you. (Having someone walk out of circle without cutting a door will make your hair stand on end, and not in a good way.)
- If you are not attending ritual but are close by, please remember a sacred event is taking place. Be quiet.
- Don't criticize the ritual or those who participate in the ritual in public. This rule means before, during or after. It is rude.
- If you have a problem with some part of the ritual or did not understand something that took place, ask the Priestess or Priest to step aside with you afterwards and discuss it *privately*. But if you just want to have a moment of ego, we suggest you forgo this.
- Do not touch someone's ritual tools without asking permission. That is not polite and you might get hurt.
- If you've never attended a public ritual, go to the Ritual 101 class that is offered. You can ask all the questions you need to at that time. You will be informed what to do, when and how to pass the chalice, what to say and how to act. You will feel much more confident and comfortable.
- If you want to bring swords or other weapons into the circle, please don't wave them around. You could put an eye out.
- Please turn off your cell phone.

◯ЅProblems and Complaints೩০
Murder is illegal.

Where do I begin? I have found that you cannot make all of the people happy all of the time, but you can make a lot of the people happy most of the time. People are going to complain; that is the nature of the beast. We live in a very negative world. You would think or hope that Pagans, given their philosophies, would be a bit different. You would like to think that we are more accepting, more able to "go with the flow," more Zen. And many of us are all of those things, but you will run into the one person at the festival who is not. If you are running the festival, don't worry about running into them; they will seek you out so they can bitch.

What do they complain about? How many stars are in the Milky Way? Most likely it will be about any number of truly unimportant things. I have been yelled at because the admission was too expensive, because we did not provide enough variety of foods for breakfast, because we had feast first and then ritual, because we had ritual first and then feast, because we chanted too long in ritual, because the merchants were too far away, because the merchants were too close and causing a traffic problem, because people did not take the spiritual nature of the festival seriously enough, because there were bugs, because it was too hot, because it was too cold, because it was too wet, because there was no hot water in the showers, because there was not enough vegetarian fare at feast, because the drummers were too loud, because there were not enough drummers, because water was too wet and rocks were too hard. At the first festival we did, I was fussed at because a late arrival was incensed that we did not have a half-day price. (Quite frankly, given the cheap price we were charging, I had not even thought of that. I refunded half her money.) The list goes on and on. It can make you crazy! Don't let it.

Most complaints will probably be trivial to you, but you must remember that it is very important to the complainer. Just remember as you stand there listening to someone complain because she was not allowed to put her tent on the ritual field and had to move it, most of the people who come to your festival will have a great time and will love and bless you for the effort.

    You must also remember that you are a professional in this situation. The buck stops with you, no matter what. You have to remove all your personal feelings for the people involved. You must be Spock-like. That takes some doing, especially for me; I am very un-Spock-like. I am a hothead from the word go. Despite that, I try to keep my cool. When a person brings you a complaint, you must first ascertain if the complaint poses a danger to anyone at the festival. Does it involve fire, flood, wild animals or wild children running amok? If it does, then you attend to the problem immediately. If it is not an emergency, assure the complainer that you will see to the problem and fix it, if that is at all possible.

    There are always problem that you did not foresee, and people will complain. One year dinner was late because we cooked pigs over a fire pit, and it took a little longer to prepare the food. There were some snide remarks about that. But, really, it is hard to complain when your mouth is full, and I did not see anyone turn down his or her share of pig. A side note here: we never did find all of the pig heads. There should have been five and we only found four. No one ever complained about that, and I have tried not to lose sleep over it.

    You will have complaints about your staff. Especially if a staff member tells a festivalgoer to stop doing something or that they can't do something. Check out the situation yourself. Mostly I have to side with my staff member because the complaint usually has something to do with the rules. If that is the case, explain the rules, and tell the complainer that you are sure they want to comply. Sometimes a festivalgoer will be just plain rude to a staff member because they are the "help." In that case, just tell the individual that the staff is there to help them, not to be a whipping boy.

    If the problem is with the staff member, apologize to the person who is upset. Then have a little "Come to Zeus" talk with the staff member. Make him/her understand that the festival is like a business; the customer always comes first. The staff is there to serve.

    I have had people grumble about the length of time we chanted. That complaint floored me; I thought getting people revved up and raising energy was fun. Everyone has different ideas, and we all learn from each other. (I keep telling myself this over and over.)

One year, three days after the festival, I received an angry email berating me because the site of the festival was not handicapped-friendly. In fact, the writer accused me of picking a site that was not handicapped accessible at all because I was anti-handicapped people. I was stunned, and then I got mad. Unfortunately for me, one usually follows hard on the heels of the other. I wrote the fellow back and asked if he had attended the festival since his name was not familiar to me. He confessed that he had not even been there. Then I got even angrier. I informed him that I do not own the state park; the state owns it. There is not a lot of money in the budget for the parks in our state, and the camp is old. I further informed him that we had requested a wheelchair ramp for the main hall building, and the ranger had built it for us because he was a nice guy. Furthermore, until Pagans pull together and raise money for our own land, we will remain at the mercy of the parks or whomever else we rent from.

I guess I chewed on him pretty good because he changed his tune. He told me that he wanted to start an organization that would work for the rights of disabled Pagans, and he intended to enlist community leaders to help him. I guess we were his first test case, and he did not do too well. I told you I am a hot head. Our site is not very handicapped-friendly, but we do the best we can and try to accommodate everyone. My staff works hard to make sure that everyone gets to where they want to go. We even have burly men that will carry people if necessary. At this point in time, that is about the best we can do, unless the state finds a bag full of money that they will give to our parks. I won't hold my breath.

If you don't have people whining or yelling at you (that is a miracle), you will have other problems. Some local covens might not come and play with you. It happened to us. One local High Priestess did not just discourage her members from attending but actually forbade them to attend. She told them that we had attendees sign a waiver and that they were signing over their souls to us with their signature. I promise you. Given the deflated prices on souls in this day and age, that was just plain silly. Really the waiver states that festival folks will not sue us if they sustain an injury or accident. There is nothing in there about souls, not even in the small print. Pagan politics, what can I say? You will have people who just won't come play with you. Suck it up. There will probably be some ugly remarks about the festival in general and you in particular. It comes with the territory. Roll with the punches and take pride in a job well done.

One year, one of my best helpers did not show up. She and her husband were divorcing, and it was an ugly divorce. He made sure to tell her that he would be at the festival with his new girlfriend, the one he had been cheating on her with during the marriage. She knew they were only coming to cause a scene, and she did not wish to play that game. She told me about it beforehand so I was not left hanging, bless her heart, but I sure missed her help. It was awkward socially too because I had to be civil to the ex. Oh well, when you are working with humans, sometimes personal stuff like this happens. While we are on this subject, there will probably be people who attend your festival that you don't like. You cannot play favorites, and you must be civil to everyone. Some days that is tougher than others.

There will be an injury, which is why we have our very own EMT. One year, a little boy ran face first into a metal pole just after his mother had told him not to run in the dark. He sustained two black eyes from that. We have had bee stings and splinters and sunburn. Our injury list has been small, thanks to the gods. I want to keep it that way. But when you have a lot of folks in the woods in the dark and playing with fire, the odds are good someone is going to hurt themselves. Be ready for it.

You will have drunks and people who think they should fire walk (usually the same people). Do the best you can with them; drunk people are hard to reason with. We have been pretty lucky with this. There has been drinking; it is impossible to enforce a "No Drinking Rule." But no one has gotten out of hand. They just seem to want to sing loudly and then pass out. Okay by me.

You will be using fire. We learned that we need buckets of sand or water by the labyrinth in case of fire. It is much easier to throw sand or water on a grass fire than to have twenty people running around stomping it out. Not as funny maybe, but probably safer. One year, people who did not want to go to bed kept throwing wood in the bonfire. When they finally wandered off to sleep, they left the fire burning. We have put a last-call for firewood on the bonfire now, so that we do not have a smoldering fire at daylight.

Some of your Big-Nose Witches will annoy the hell out of you because they are Big-Nose Witches. 'Nuff said.

I will never cease to be amazed at some of the dumb things that people want to do. For instance, we do not allow drugs at PUF. Yet, I had a person approach me to complain about that policy. It seems that this person could not get through a whole day without a joint. Now, if you cannot get through the day without dope, you have a much bigger problem than I am equipped to solve. So the answer was no. That person stayed home.

An individual approached me and offered to do a workshop on the kundalini. The workshop was for couples, and there would be sexual activity involved. I thanked her kindly for her offer and told her we had all the classes we needed. I try not to be a prude, but we run a family-oriented festival in a state park. That was a headache I did not need. People are welcome to raise their kundalini however they see fit, as long as it does not involve small children or little furry animals, and they do it in the privacy of their tent or cabin. I just did not think that raising it in the main hall while we were trying to cook lunch was a good idea…probably not sanitary either.

People want to have fires outside their cabins despite the fact that it clearly states in the rules that fires are not permitted except in the two designated areas. They want to argue about this. It is not my rule, it is the park rule, and the rangers would freak out. We try to ensure that never happens since they have guns.

We have had people leave their children unattended while they went to drum circle—little kids under the age of two. The people who have done this have assured me that it was fine because their child slept in a port-a-crib, and they left them asleep. I assured the individuals that if it happened again, I would call the police myself right after I had finished beating their ass.

Every year someone demands to know why we do not allow swimming in the lake. And every year I explain to them about the snapping turtles in the lake. They always promise to take their chances. One of these days I will lose my temper and throw someone in the damn lake. Let's see how they feel about snapping turtles then!

We always get someone who wants to come into the kitchen and cook their own food because they have special dietary needs. It really is not

Problems and Complaints

possible. The kitchen is a mad house in the time leading up to meals. We can't afford the space for them, and we can't have people who are not helping out with the main meal under foot.

There are always folks that beg to come to the site early so they may set up. Some people have requested to come a day early. It sounds like a simple thing, but if you let one person do that, where do you draw the line? If you don't draw the line, you will have a campsite full of folks before you can get set up and be ready for them.

We have had a couple of kid problems. We had a teenager who would not keep her ID bracelet on. The reason we make teenagers wear the ID bracelet is so that other folks will know that they are underage and will not act inappropriately toward them. The teen was spoken to several times. She developed an attitude and was finally escorted to her family encampment and told to stay there. The real problem was that the parent thought that I was unfair to her child and had not provided enough entertainment for teenagers. I can tell you, that is not the reaction my mother would have had if I had been dragged home after midnight at fourteen. My only answer to the situation was to tell the woman that she and her child could cross PUF off their list of festivals to attend.

Another time, we had packs of kids roaming the site looking for something to do. That, in and of itself, is not a bad thing. I did lots of roaming as a kid. But someone got pushed into the lake, and that was scary. The other thing that happened was that one child pulled a knife on another child and threatened him. Now, the child in question was under the age of ten. My answer to the problem was to gather all the children involved and their parents and read them the Riot Act à la Tish. That involves me explaining to the children that I will not put up with any such nonsense under any circumstances and that if anything even close to this happened again, I would fall on them like a house. I yelled, I threatened, and I told them that on the site of PUF, I was God, and if they got out of line again, no one would be able to save them from me. I further explained that I was chaining them to their parents, and I had better not see them wandering again for the rest of the weekend. I then sent them to bed. I confiscated the knife too.

Harsh? You betcha. No one endangers children on my watch, even another child. Some of the parents did not particularly like my safety talk. But one of the rules of running a festival is that you are the Boss, period, end of story, and everyone has to understand that. I don't like yelling at little kids and making them cry—no really, I don't, no matter what anyone tells you. But they needed to understand that I would not put up with insane behavior and that I would be watching them.

I could have thrown them all off site, but I decided not to do that. It was late, and it would have been a long drive back into the city on dark country roads. So I opted to scare the hell out of them instead. It was a tough call to make, but luckily it worked out fine. There was no more trouble from the kids involved in the unpleasant incident, and all the other children walked small for the rest of the weekend. There was peace in the land, and it was good.

There is a new problem in the Pagan community that I have been hearing about for a few years now—the pedophile. The people who bring their children to your festival expect them to be safe, and they deserve to be safe. We have the attitude that at a festival of like-minded people, the children will be safe from harm. We kind of watch them, but they mostly run free and play and have fun. The children interact with the adults and vice-versa because for the most part, we like children. The children have been taught to beware of strangers, but at a festival there are no strangers. It is a perfect place for a pedophile to find the opportunity to harm a child. These people talk to each other, and I can assure you that the word has gotten out on the Pagan festival.

What can we do to protect our children? First, the parents have to do their part and watch their kids. They need to know where they are at all times, and never leave them unattended. They have to watch and see whom their children are talking to and who is talking to them.

As an organizer you have to do your part and keep you eyes open. Don't be naive. If you hear a rumor about someone, check it out, find out the truth. If you find the rumor to be true, you can refuse the person in question admission if they show up. Or, if you find out after they are already on site, throw them off your site. Yes, you can do that; it is your festival. Don't just hope that nothing bad will happen, take action. You are responsible.

You have to see who shows a more than passing interest in your children, and ask questions. You have to listen to the talk that flows through the festival. You have to listen when a child or a parent comes to you and tells you that someone on your site has made them uncomfortable.

You have to have a good staff that will watch any person who you suspect is questionable. And you must have the balls to eject a person from your site if you think that their actions or interactions with children are inappropriate.

Have I had to do this? Yes I have, and I will do it again if necessary. I would rather that the word go out on the pedophile network that PUF is a tough nut to crack, don't bother.

We have instituted a new plan to help keep our children safe. Up until now we have made all minors wear an armband that has their name, parent's name and cabin number on it. This is information that we have decided needs to be kept private. So in the future, every child will wear an armband with a code number on it. That code number will be on a list containing all the info. That list will be under lock and key. The number will be picked randomly. We also have daycare for our children where they are under the eyes of staff members, not roaming around site alone. We intend to make it difficult for anyone who would try to harm any of our children.

You will spend a lot of time enforcing the rules. That is just a fact of life. Be nice but firm, and don't let anyone run over you. If someone gives you a real problem, show him or her the door. I have had to be a bitch (I know that is hard to believe) when problems got out of hand. People did not like it, but they did get over it. Grow a thick skin; you will need it.

This chapter may sound like all you have is problems, which is certainly not the case. The good things far outweigh the bad. That is why I keep doing it year after year. I intend to be doing PUF on a walker and dragging an oxygen tank behind me.

❃Things You Need To Bring❃
Hammers, saws and drain cleaner

This is an all-inclusive list, and no matter your site or circumstances, you will be able to amend it to your needs. No matter how well you plan, you will forget something come the day of the festival, I promise. Find a willing victim and send him/her out to the local we-got-everything store.

A
- Anti-bacterial wipes — For kitchens and baths, these make clean up so much faster and easier!

B
- Batteries
- Bug spray

C
- Change
- Citronella candles
- Coffeemaker

D
- Duct tape
- Drink container, large insulated kind — more than one if you can. You can have several different kinds of drinks to offer at the same time. Makes it easier to brew up more tea or whatever as well. You can empty one and replace it with the other.
- Dish scrubbing sponges
- Drain cleaner
- Dish towels

E
- Extra blankets — especially if you live in a place where the weather is unpredictable, like Tennessee. One year at PUF, the temperature dropped during the night, and we all almost froze. I handed out all the extra socks from my bag to my cabin mates.

Things You Need To Bring

F
- First-aid kit
- Flashlight

G
- Glue — add a couple of extra kinds such as Elmer's, Super and maybe plastic cement. You can bet that you will use one kind or another before the weekend is out. Murphy's law #13: Something that is vital and irreplaceable will always break when you are in the woods and far from civilization.
- Games

H
- Hammer — oh so many uses. But really, if you are camping you will need it for pounding tent pegs and sometimes repairing the old windows, doors and whatnot in the camp.

I
- ID method

J
- Jellybeans

K
- Knives — for kitchen

L
- Light bulbs
- Light sources for camp common areas — These can be lanterns, torches, pots o' citronella or candles in glass containers.
- Lost & Found Box — Put this someplace in the common area where everyone will see it.

M
- Moneybox
- Money

N
- Nuts — Oh never mind, they will show up on their own.

O
- Oven mitts

P
- Paper
- Pins
- Pots
- Pans
- Pens
- Platters to serve
- Pitchers
- Poster board for signs
- Paper towels
- Pliers
- Prizes

Q
- Quidditch set

R
- Rope
- Rain gear

S
- Sunscreen — extra sunscreen because someone will forget theirs. And you need it even on a cloudy day.
- Staple gun — Again so many uses, but really they are great for putting up signs—much better than tape (which peels off) or nails (which are hard to remove).
- Soap
- Signs — to indicate tenting, merchants, workshop and where the site is, etc.
- Sewing kit
- Scissors

T
- Toilet paper — more than you ever dreamed you would buy
- Trash bags —ditto. We hand them out at the gate and ask attendees to clean up after themselves. Remember that

even environmentally conscious Pagans can still generate a lot of trash.
- Tape — duct, masking, electrical and invisible

U

- Umbrellas

V

- Valium (just kidding)

W

- Waivers for the pay-at-the-gate folks
- Wet wipes
- Walkie-talkies — Let me rave about this for a minute. The best money ever spent in the entire history of money was what we spent on walkie-talkies. They saved about a million steps and kept us in constant communication. Plus they are a lot of fun to play with at night after the camp is asleep (seems some of us do not get out enough). We buy the ones with a 2-mile radius. Check out that range for yourself. They don't really get out that far, given the hilly terrain in Tennessee. But the range is sufficient for our needs. Buy some; you will not be sorry!

X

- I tried, but I came up empty.

Y

- Yo-yos — no really

Z

- Zipper-type plastic bags

⋙Things They Need To Bring⋘
Don't leave home without it.

It is a long list, but if your folks are going to be comfortable in the wilds, they will need to bring much of civilization with them. Not all of the things listed are totally necessary, of course. They can come with an old sheet and one pair of clean underwear, but they won't be comfortable. The things that we require our festival folks to bring are in bold. Your folks can use it as a checklist when they are packing. Add or delete as you feel necessary. Just remember if it gets cold, you will be the person that folks will come to for extra socks.

A
- Air mattress — not really necessary, but you won't be sorry
- Antibacterial towelettes

B
- Bug spray
- Batteries
- Battery operated lantern — If you bring candles, they must be in glass containers.
- Banner — to identify yourself or your group
- Blankets
- Bedding — sleeping bags, pads, pillows, sheets, etc.

C
- Clothing — warm-weather as well as cool-weather clothing for the length of your stay. The weather varies greatly in the spring!
- Camp chair
- Comb and/or brush

D
- Drinks — plenty of water and other drinks. Tea and coffee are provided at meals.
- Doormat — useful in front of your tent to keep from tracking in too much dirt
- Deodorant

Things They Need To Bring

E
- Ever Clear (still kidding)

F
- **Feast Gear** — plates, forks, spoons, cups, etc. Be a good Pagan and don't bring disposable feast gear. There will be a "Washing Station" on the porch of the Main Hall for your convenience!
- Food — 1 bread contribution (example: 1 loaf of bread or bag of rolls) — 1 fruit or vegetable contribution — 1 covered dish contribution (example: a casserole, salad or dessert that will serve a small portion to a minimum of 25 people.*For casseroles or salads, a 9x13 pan would do this). This contribution should be in a disposable aluminum container.

G
- Grill — if you want to cook your own meals
- Glasses, prescription and sun

H
- Hammer — for tent stakes
- Hat — to keep the rain off your head, good especially if it is cold
- Hand and body lotion

I
- Ice chest

J
- Juice
- Jacket

K
- Kites

L
- Lunch stuff and snacks for in-between meals
- Lip balm

M
- Musical instruments — drums, bells, rain sticks, etc.

N
- No non-prescription drugs

O
- Only prescription drugs

P
- Personal Necessities — (Chocolate falls into this category.) Basically, bring what you need to make you comfortable for a weekend away from home.
- Prescription medications (Please be sure to bring the prescriptions in labeled bottles.)

Q
- Quarters

R
- Rain Gear (just in case!)
- Ritual gear

S
- Sunscreen
- Shoes — Bring extra in case the ones you are wearing get wet.
- Sanitizing hand gel
- Socks, extra
- Soap
- Shampoo and conditioner

T
- Tent (if tent camping!)
- Towels
- Tarp — Use it as a porch in front of your tent to provide a dry area, or in case your tent is not waterproofed, or for any number of things.
- Table, the folding camp type
- Toothbrush, toothpaste, mouthwash, floss

U
- Umbrella

V
- Vaseline

W
- Windbreaker

X
- Nope-sorry, still nothing

Y
- Yellow submarine

Z
- Zest for life!

These are only some of the items that you may wish to bring. Please make sure that you bring the things that will keep you comfortable and safe.

☙How To Buy Food☙
Measure twice, cut once.

This is a daunting task, or at least it seems so. With planning, it is not too bad. But before we get to the meat (sorry, couldn't help myself) of this issue, let me explain some facts to you. If you are going to serve food, you have to do it right. You have to give your folks lots of food—food that tastes good. And you must have lots of variety. You have to serve it when you say you are going to serve it. I know sometimes things happen that you can't control. The year of the pig roast, dinner was late, but we gave it our best shot and tried to be on time.

You have to make sure you have enough food. God help you if you run out before everyone has made it through the chow line. So err on the side of buying too much. You can always find a place for the leftovers to go. One year we served tacos, and I thought that we had made plenty. We had cooked forty pounds of hamburger. But I was wrong, so halfway through serving, I was scrambling in the kitchen to fill the gap. Luckily for me, we had several cans of chicken that had been bought for lunch; I whipped it up with taco seasoning, heated it in the microwave and served it. But I did give in to panic. Hungry Pagans can be mean Pagans.

The food you serve has to taste good. You cannot put an inexperienced person in charge of your kitchen. Just because someone is a good cook, and her or his family likes the food they cook, does not mean this person can figure out how to feed 200 people well or on time. Recipes can't just be doubled or tripled depending on how many you are feeding. They have to be played with, and tasted and stirred. This is the one time you will find out that your mother was wrong; you must play with your food. You have to trust your kitchen person. So the first thing is to find someone who can really cook, and someone who has cooked for large groups of folks. Work out menus with your cook, and have some practice dinners long before you get to festival. Fine-tune the food so there will be no surprises come festival. Discuss budget because this is where you are going to really spend money.

This is a very important job. Believe it or not, it may be the most important job of your festival. People will remember the food. You can have mediocre classes and lackluster rituals, but if you feed folks well, they will go out and tell everyone how great your event was. You can have killer workshops and rituals with the gods themselves standing quarters, but if the food is lousy, that is all that anyone will remember. You need someone who really knows his/her way around a kitchen and someone who is not afraid to give orders. Not a shy retiring person for this job. It requires planning, telling folks what to do and running folks out of the kitchen that don't belong in there. Ask Dorothy Morrison.

If you say that you are going to serve breakfast, for gods' sakes have your act together. You don't want people wandering into the kitchen looking for food and finding none. That may mean you can't party the night before. It may mean that your staff can't party either. Or you can set up a simple breakfast the night before. Lay out packages of oatmeal, loaves of bread, jelly and some fruit. Put a note on the coffee maker that says "Turn me on," and go have fun. This may not be a perfect answer, but at least food will be available. Don't disappoint your guests.

Now that I have scared the hell out of you about cooking and serving food, let's get on with it. First you have to have a good idea how many people are coming to the festival. That is one of the reasons that we do pre-registration. Our reservation number is usually about half of our gate, so we figure accordingly. This may or may not hold true for you; it is a figure you have to play with. There are usually less folks to feed on the first night or nights of festival than on the last night. Now I realize that our festival is the social event of the season, but not everyone can take off two days from work, and we plan accordingly. We look at our numbers the week of the festival and figure food needs.

We do a simple meal on the first night, one that can be kept warm for a long period of time. People are arriving all hours of the day and night, and they appreciate a warm meal. We have a couple of different kinds of soups in crock-pots, bread, cheese, fruit, tea, lemonade and coffee. Soup is easy to make, it is cheap; it can be made early in the day and kept warm till midnight. Perfect. We make one non-vegetarian soup and one vegetarian soup so that everyone is happy. At this point, we are making ten gallons of soup for Thursday night. This guarantees that everyone will have a bowl of soup, maybe two, and there will be some left over. If there is any left over, that is not a problem. We stick it in the fridge and serve it for lunch the next day. We set out all the food we are serving and leave it so that folks can wander in and serve themselves. On the first night, we allow folks to come into the kitchen to wash their plates and accoutrements because we are not busy in there. We break it all down and clean up before we go to bed, lay out anything that does not need to be refrigerated for breakfast and fill the coffee makers.

The second night, we do an easy dinner, usually spaghetti or tacos, or baked potatoes, salad, fruit, bread, dessert, tea, lemonade and coffee. We have a set time for dinner and cry the camp to let everyone know that dinner is served. There is not a huge variety of food, but there is plenty and everyone eats their fill. This meal is served chow-line style.

We have finally set the chow line up so that it moves quickly; we don't want people fainting in line from hunger—or grumbling. We set the food up on the tables, and people move down the line picking the foods they want to eat. Staff members stand on the opposite side of the table and encourage folks to only take as much food as they can eat, assuring them that there is plenty and that they can come back for seconds. This can take a bit of time depending on how many folks you have attending, but I think that we have a system now that works pretty well. Believe me, we did it wrong a bunch of times first.

We put the VIPs at the head of the line, and the merchants are right behind them. You have to treat your VIPs special because they are. The merchants need to eat quickly so that they can get back to their booths. Everyone else comes after them, and then last but not least, the long-suffering (and starving) staff eats.

The last night of festival we have the Big Feast. The tables groan with the weight of the food, and folks eat until they are stuffed like turkeys. It is great! This meal is also served chow-line style.

We set a breakfast spread each morning that starts at 7:30 A.M. This means we don't have to get up at "Oh-Dark-Thirty" to cook, and everyone still has plenty of time to eat before the first class of the day starts. I believe that folks have to be fed well at breakfast time; they have a big day ahead of them after all. Breakfast usually consists of individual packs of dry cereal, individual packs of oatmeal, yogurt, granola, fruit, toast and jam, coffee and orange juice. It is a lot of food that will carry you through the day, and we don't have to kill ourselves cooking.

One year, we had a donation of ten pounds of oatmeal. The slow cooking kind. If you have never cooked enough oatmeal to feed a small starving nation, let me tell you it is quite a treat. We cooked it in big five-gallon pots and stood over it and stirred and stirred and stirred. By the time we were done, I felt like a kitchen wench from the twelfth century—and looked like it too, I might add. But, it was free and that was good, and oatmeal really sticks to the old ribs. If you add enough sugar, milk, honey and whatnot to it, it actually tastes pretty good too.

Another year, we had a donation of about a million cinnamon rolls and an equal number of breakfast burritos (it is good to have friends in low places), and that really was a treat. We ate like kings.

We offer lunch, but it costs extra. The reason we sell lunch is because not everyone wants to stay on site for lunch; they want to get off site for a time. We can't gauge how many to prepare for, and so this is our answer to the problem. We sell lunch tickets, so we know exactly how many lunches to prepare. Lunch consists of tuna or chicken or egg salad, fruit, chips, cookies or brownies, and of course, tea, lemonade and coffee. Folks come in, show their tickets and take their lunch. No muss, no fuss. This has become the job of the teenagers and Beth. They all seem to like doing it—we don't know why, but it gives the rest of us a break.

On Sunday morning, which is the last day of the festival, we lay out all the leftovers and folks chow down. We bag up and box up the remains and send it all to the appointed places where it will do some good.

For the past couple of years, we have had entertainment during dinner. It occupies the folks that are standing in line who would otherwise be bored. Plus, it adds a festive air. Let me say here, before your minds go to other places, that the entertainment is musical!

We encourage folks to bring their own dishes to save a little wear and tear on the environment. Yeah, yeah, it is that whole nature religion thing. We set up a dish-washing stand on the front or back porch with hot soapy water and hot rinse water. There is a trashcan, so folks can scrape their plates and bowls before they go into the water. The line gets a little long here as well, but folks are very good-natured about it. On the site that we use, we must heat the water and haul it to the porch. It is not fun, but that is what kitchen wenches are for.

We provide all of the food for dinner on Thursday and Friday as well as breakfast and lunch. For the Saturday evening meal, we ask that each festivalgoer bring bread, a bag of fruit and a casserole. We provide the meat. People are amazing, and the food they bring knocks my socks off every year. We always have dozens of different kinds of salads, every kind and combination of casserole both with meat and without, veggies, desserts, mouth-watering homemade dishes and lots of homemade bread as well. We also have lots of frozen lasagnas from the grocery store, and that is good too. We think that the more food the merrier. One year, we did have twenty-seven frozen lasagnas in the freezer. We laughed and figured *"Bring Lasagna"* must have been out there on the psychic wavelength. But we ate them all.

On Saturday evening, we leave the food out until midnight, so that anyone who needs a snack won't have to go hunting for it. Plus, we figure that the more folks eat, the less left over for us to have to deal with. Before you get all worried that we might poison our folks this way, please know that it is cool in Tennessee at night in Spring. I would not do this if our festival took place in August.

Our staff works in the kitchen, but they have other duties as well. So we use our volunteers in the kitchen too (the aforementioned kitchen wenches). We sit down and figure out the schedule for each day of the festival and count up how many volunteers we need for each 1.5 hour time block. We need only a few folks for the breakfast setup, and many times the staff handles that without any help. We need a few more for lunch and a bunch for the dinner prep. I give the list of necessary bodies to my volunteer person, and she signs up folks for the needed times. It is a horrible feeling to be two hours from dinner, the meal is half cooked, and you don't have enough hands to get the rest done in time. You will work yourself into the ground if you do not have enough help. Don't let this happen to you; use your volunteers. Don't forget to schedule volunteers for clean up; you will need them.

If you are fortunate enough to have refrigeration, good for you. Even so, there are precautions you need to take so you don't poison anyone. Keep everything in the fridge until you need to prepare it. Keep your kitchen clean. We use the anti-bacterial wipes. They are great for a quick clean up. If you have different kinds of meat to prepare, wipe the surface off after each prep. This is especially important if you are preparing chicken. I prepare it last as an extra precaution. Be a hand-washing Nazi.

It gets crazy in the kitchen at mealtime, so try and go with the flow. If you panic, nothing will get done in time. If you have enough help, you or the person who is the chief cook should be able to sit in a chair enjoying a boat drink while giving orders.

To figure out how much food to buy, get your estimated gate numbers and a calculator. If you are serving soup, figure eight ounces per person. Then add a bit more. I usually figure my numbers and then add ten percent extra. That way I know there will be plenty. Remember that Pagans can really eat under normal circumstances. The Pagans you will be serving have been playing in the woods all day, and they have built up an appetite!

The same goes for breakfast. Figure your numbers and buy accordingly. Figure one bowl of cereal or oatmeal per person. Buy the institution size of jelly or jam, and use some of your donated bread for the toast. If you are serving fruit, cut it up as you go so it won't turn brown. For some reason, folks won't seem to eat uncut fruit except for bananas, so get a knife. We make coffee in the huge urns; we have two of them, so we don't run out. There is nothing more pitiable than a sleep deprived Pagan standing sadly by the coffee maker with a cup waiting. We serve Tang, and we make that in a five-gallon dispenser.

We figure our lunch based on how many we sold the year before. We buy the institutional size cans of tuna and chicken—several more than we think that we will need in case we have a lunch rush. If we buy too much, it keeps. We put our lunch components (sandwiches, cookies, etc.) in sandwich bags, and it all goes into brown paper bags.

For the evening meals, there is a rule of thumb for how much to prepare. The average meal in America is a ¼ pound hamburger with lettuce, tomato and cheese, a large fry, a turnover and a large drink. You are serving Pagans so up that amount a little more. For meat that is sliced to serve, such as ham, roast beef, pork loin, etc., figure six ounces per person. For chicken on the bone, figure eight ounces per person. Do the math on that and translate it to pounds. I realize that kids will eat less, and you will have some vegetarians, but if you use this as a guide, you will have plenty of meat.

Figure out your menu months in advance, and make a list that includes everything you need to prepare the dishes you will be serving. That includes things like the milk needed to make the potato soup. Don't trust it to memory, write it down!

Meat goes on sale from time to time; watch the ads in the paper. Buy it cheap and freeze it. Remove it from the store packages first, wrap it in foil and put it in zipper-type freezer bags. This prevents freezer burn. When you thaw it to cook, it will be as good as the day you bought it.

While we are talking about buying, let me add this note. Don't just make a food list; make a list of everything you will need, things like toilet paper, paper towels, lights bulbs, etc. Look at the sale ads every week and catch things on sale. Encourage your staff to do the same. Let them help you spot the bargains. Remind them to check with you before they buy. Find a place to stockpile everything and buy, buy, buy.

Buying whole veggies to cut up for soups is cheaper than buying them canned or frozen. It is a lot of trouble, but remember that you will have help in the kitchen. Twenty-five pounds of potatoes is cheap and it really stretches.

Compare prices. Look at all the ads before you buy. You may think that the chicken at Mo's Road-Kill Grocery and Bait Shop is the best buy in town, but you may be wrong. Talk to the butcher at the store and tell him what you need; you may be able to get a better deal because you are buying in bulk. If anyone has a friend in the restaurant business, you might be able to buy wholesale. Don't just jump into the car the week of the festival and go to the local big box grocery store. You will save money if you plan ahead.

You want to get the best prices you can for the food you buy, but you still want quality. Try and resist the idea of serving a lot of something just because it is cheap. I went to an event one time, and they served carrots (really cheap) in everything and cooked every way imaginable. They were still carrots. I don't remember anything else about that event. See what I mean?

Don't worry about buying too much of the dry items; most of it will keep if you use zipper-type plastic bags and put everything in plastic tubs. We buy tea in the big family-size tea bag boxes. We go through a lot of it. Teabags will keep if stored properly, so it does not go to waste. We buy coffee in the huge cans and the same for the lemonade. We buy twenty-five pounds of sugar, and we use all of it. I think that small nations do not use as much sugar as we do. If we have any coffee or sugar left over, it won't keep, but we can find a place for it to go. You can too.

We buy lots of zipper-type plastic bags and big industrial rolls of aluminum foil to store the leftovers in. It is cheaper that way. Everything left over goes into the bags to preserve freshness.

We are fortunate in that we have a great kitchen to use. We can cook tons of food all at one time. We start heating up the casseroles on Saturday afternoon, cover them in foil and put them on top of each other to retain the heat. They are warm for dinner. For the dishes that need to be served hot, we have a system. We have wire holders that big aluminum pans fit into; we put a pan into them and fill the pan about ¼ full of hot water. Then we put the food into another disposable aluminum pan and set it in the bottom pan. We put sterno under that to keep the food warm. With the water as the buffer, nothing gets crunchy. You can buy these in a restaurant supply house, and sometimes you will find them in the big box stores.

If you are setting the food out in a chow line, which I recommend, put the food out in this order: bread, salads, veggies, casseroles and put the meat last. Usually folks are hungry by dinnertime, and their eyes are bigger than their stomachs. If you put the food in this order, they will fill their plates with all the other food before they get to the meat, and they will not take too much. If you put the meat out first, no matter how well you have planned, you will run out.

So what if you figure dinner for 100 and you get 150? Don't panic. You will know this figure long before you have to serve the food if you keep in touch with the person on your front gate. Get a constant update on the numbers coming in. If that peaks over the number you have prepared for, send someone to the store. If the food trip is early enough in the day, you can just get more of what you are serving and cook it up. If the food run is at the eleventh hour, have your gopher get food that is already cooked. You can handle this. Just keep a cool head.

You will probably have food left over—always better to have too much than too little. What do you do with it? Check around with your guests. There may be someone on site who could use a bit of extra food themselves, or they might know someone who can. Some of the leftovers will be just that, pieces and parts of casseroles, and some will be entire loaves of bread and sacks of apples. Two entirely different problems. Some soup kitchens will take the leftover casseroles, many won't. We give our casseroles to a lady who manages a Section 8 apartment building. She takes all the leftovers home with her, warms it all up for the folks who live in the complex, and they have a big dinner. Our routine now is to put all the leftovers in zipper-type plastic bags for easy handling and freeze them. We find someone who needs it and deliver it still frozen. It is a great solution. Look around and see who is willing to take leftovers in your area; check with homeless shelters and battered-women shelters. Our packaged, unopened food, fruit and bread go to the Martha O'Bryan Center in Nashville, TN. They are located in a low-income housing development, and they have many wonderful programs for the folks who live there. They also hand out food to help those food stamp dollars stretch. They are always happy to see us come with a carload of bread and fruit. I get a love letter from them every year. It makes me feel all warm and gooey inside.

The kitchen we use has big walk-in coolers and a walk-in freezer. We put all the food we bring in the fridge—and all of the food that our festivalgoers bring as well. We are very fortunate. What do you do if you don't have such a set-up? If you are using a primitive site without refrigeration, you can still pull off a great feast. Many things can be cooked in advance and frozen. You can put the food in a cooler, carry it all to site, then set the food out and let it thaw. It won't be warm for dinner, but it won't kill anyone either. (An important consideration in my book.) You can cook ham, roast beef or pork roasts, and they will make the trip just fine. Plus, they taste fine cold. Barbecue is just as good hot as cold, and most folks love it. Tons of potato salad can be made, put into zipper-type plastic bags and stashed in the coolers. You need lots of ice for anything that can spoil, so check the coolers often to see how much melt you have. You can grill chicken, but you must be careful. Buy the chicken the day you intend to serve it. Give yourself enough lead-time to get it cooked, plus the travel time to and from the store, and send someone out to buy it. Put it on the fire as soon as it gets in your hands. You can keep it warm and lessen the chance of spoilage by putting it in the coolers after it is cooked. Line a cooler with foil, then put an open garbage bag in on top of that. As the chicken comes off the grill, toss it into the cooler. It will be warm and wonderful for your evening meal. Ice chests are great; they keep the cold stuff cold and the hot stuff hot—how do they know? Beats me, I don't understand color television either.

You can also cook whole pigs; we have done it. Man oh man, was it good! But, it is a hot job, and it takes hours to get the meat thoroughly cooked. But if you are brave, don't mind sweating (or lost pig heads), and can find a pig farmer who will dress them out for you, I say go for it.

There are a couple of other solutions to food. One is to not serve food at all and have folks bring their own food. This makes the price of festival cheaper for you, and you have a lot less work. Plus, if someone gets food poisoning, it's not your fault. Another idea is to allow food vendors to come and offer their wares to your folks. The festivalgoer pays them. You can charge the vendor or not, and that is up to you. Or you can charge for meals.

If you are going to have independent food merchants at your event, the food they serve must be really good and reasonably priced. Get referrals, and if possible, go to an event where these folks are cooking and taste their wares.

When all is said and done, there are just a few rules to follow. Stick to a budget, get your menus drawn up, buy as cheap as you can, get the best quality you can, make a lot, make it good, get lots of help, delegate and plan, plan, plan. See, easy as pie.

Recipes
Yum! Yum!

These are some tried and true recipes from PUF. They are fairly cheap to make, taste good, and they are not work intensive. I have included meat thermometer directions for many of the dishes, but if you don't have one, you can check for doneness by sinking a sharp knife into the meat. If the knife goes in easily, the meat is ready. If you make more of any dish than I have indicated, don't just double the spices used. Taste as you add, so you do not over spice the dish. Please note that all herbs and seasonings are listed as a guide, you may season the dishes to your taste.

GLOP

This is for the kids to munch on during the day. It is cheap and easy to make and does not need to be refrigerated.

1 box honey & nut flavored oat cereal O's
1 box bite-size crispy wheat cereal squares
1 box bite-size crispy rice cereal squares
1 large package of stick pretzels
1 package mini marshmallows
1 large package chocolate chips
1 large package dried fruit (bananas are the best)

Toss all the ingredients into a large plastic bowl with a tight-fitting lid. Stir all the ingredients together, put the lid on, and it is ready to serve. You can serve it in small paper cups, and the kids can carry it around with them. Give the container a good shake before you start serving.

MEAT PIES

2 frozen pie crusts
1 can mushroom soup
½ pound hamburger
¼ cup of shredded cheese
1 tablespoon sour cream
¼ teaspoon salt
¼ teaspoon pepper
¼ teaspoon powdered garlic
1 tablespoon butter
½ teaspoon sugar
¼ teaspoon cinnamon

Brown one pie shell just slightly (poke holes in it first). Fry the hamburger, drain well and set aside. Mix the mushroom soup, sour cream, salt, pepper and garlic together and add to the hamburger. Mix well. Spoon the contents into the browned pie shell, fill it but don't overfill it. Sprinkle the shredded cheese on the hamburger mixture. Put the uncooked pie shell on top; brush melted butter on that and sprinkle with sugar and cinnamon. Cut slits in the pie shell. Bake for approximately 45 minutes at 350°F. This is one dish that will freeze and travel well. If that is what you intend to do, allow the pie to cool completely. Wrap it in aluminum foil and pop it in a freezer bag. You can stack them on top of each other in the freezer. Put them in an ice chest to transport them. Set them out to thaw early; they take a while to defrost. They are great cold. Or you can warm them up in an oven at 300°F for about 30 minutes.

Each pie will serve 8 people—or 4 really hungry people.

ROAST PIG

1 dressed pig, (don't be silly, you know what I mean) usually weighs about 12 pounds
large bowl
brush for basting
1 teaspoon salt
½ teaspoon pepper
1 cup honey
1 cup brown sugar
1 can cola
1 stick of butter

Make a fire, and when you have coals, lay the pig on the grill. Mix the salt, pepper, honey, brown sugar, butter and cola in a pan and stir well, and place this on the grill. Stir as the butter melts. Brush the mixture on the pig, flip him and brush the other side. Continue to brush the mixture on the pig as he cooks. The cook time will vary, depending on your fire and the size of the pig. He needs to be turned often so that he will be cooked thoroughly. Use a meat thermometer and allow the pig to cook until the temp. reaches 150°F. When the pig is done, let it cool for about an hour and then slice it off the bone.

You can also purchase an injector and inject the glaze mixture under the skin. This makes the work easier, but the pig still has to be turned often.

Ask the person who supplies the pig how much it weighs, and figure about 8 ounces of meat for each person.

ROAST GOAT

1 dressed goat
large bowl
brush for basting
clove of garlic
stick of butter
1 small onion
½ cup mint leaves—chopped and bruised
1 teaspoon salt
1 teaspoon pepper

Make a fire, and when you have coals, lay the goat on the grill. Mix the garlic, butter, chopped onion, chopped mint leaves, salt and pepper in a pan, and place this on the grill. Stir as the butter melts. Brush the mixture on the goat, flip him and brush the other side. Continue to brush the mixture on the goat as he cooks. The cook time will vary, depending on your fire and the size of the goat. He needs to be turned often so that he will be cooked thoroughly—about every 15 or 20 minutes. Use a meat thermometer and allow the goat to cook until the temp. reaches 180°F. A small goat should take about an hour or so to cook completely. Goat can be a little tough; the younger the goat, the more tender you will find it. Don't cook it to death, or it will be even tougher. You can even serve it a bit pink if you like. When the goat is done, let it cool for about an hour, and then slice it off the bone.

Ask the person who supplies the goat how much it weighs, and figure about 8 ounces of meat for each person.

ROAST TURKEY

1 boneless turkey roast (I know it is more money, but you don't have bone, and you get more bang for your buck)
large bowl
brush or turkey baster
1 teaspoon salt
1 teaspoon pepper
1 cup orange juice
1 teaspoon sage

Slice the meat before you cook it. It will cook faster, and you will get the basting mixture on every piece. Place the meat in a pan. Mix the salt, pepper, orange juice and sage in a bowl and pour it over the meat. Bake it in an oven for approximately 2 hours at 350°F. Use the turkey baster to spread the mixture over the meat about every 15 minutes to keep the meat moist.

We have cooked turkey in the large electric roasters, and that works great. Slice it, place it in the roaster, coat it with the basting mixture and cover. Cook for approx. 2 hours at 350°F, or whatever comparable temp. your roaster has. Check the meat regularly as these can sometimes cook very fast. Use the turkey baster to spread the mixture over the meat about every 15 minutes to keep the meat moist.

You can also leave the turkey roast whole and cook it over a fire. Take a sharp knife and insert it in the roast as far as it will go; do this all over the roast. Let it sit in the basting mixture and turn it occasionally. Do this for about an hour before you cook. Place it on the grill and brush the basting mixture over it constantly. Use a meat thermometer with this method, and allow the internal temp. to reach 185°F. Slice and serve. Figure 6 ounces of meat for each person.

If you want to get fancy, use an injector and shoot the basting mixture into the bird before and during cooking. You can deep-fry the turkey. The process is fast and the meat tastes great. The drawbacks are: danger of fire and cost of peanut oil. With this method you can still inject the basting mixture before you put it into the oil.

HAM

1 boneless ham (same reason as for the turkey) of approx. 10 lbs.
1 cup honey
1 cup brown sugar
½ cup brown corn syrup
1 can cola

Slice the meat before you cook it. It will cook faster, and you will get the basting mixture on every piece. Place the meat in a pan. Mix the honey, brown sugar, syrup and cola in a bowl and pour it over the meat. Bake it in an oven for approximately 2 hours at 350°F. The basting mixture is a bit thick, so you will probably have to use a ladle to scoop it up and pour over the meat at first. As it cooks, the basting mixture will get thinner, and you will be able to use a turkey baster. Spread the basting mixture over the meat about every 15 minutes to keep the meat moist.

You can cook the ham in a large electric roaster, and that works great. Slice it, place it in the roaster, coat it with the basting mixture and cover. Cook for approximately 2 hours at 350°F or whatever comparable temp. your roaster has. Check the meat regularly as these can sometimes cook very fast. Again, start with a soup ladle to pour the basting mixture over the meat, and use the turkey baster when the mixture thins out. Spread the mixture over the meat about every 15 minutes to keep the meat moist.

You can also leave the ham whole and cook it over a fire. Take a sharp knife and insert it in the ham as far as it will go; do this all over the ham. Let it sit in the basting mixture and turn it occasionally. Do this for about an hour before you cook. Place meat on the grill and brush the basting mixture over it constantly. Use a meat thermometer with this method and allow the internal temp. to reach 140°F. Slice and serve.

Figure 6 ounces per person.

FANCY CHICKEN

10 pounds whole chicken quarters
cheap white wine, the box kind is great
1 tablespoon salt
1 tablespoon pepper
1/2 tablespoon garlic for powdered or 1 whole clove
3 cups Italian breadcrumbs

Mix the salt, pepper, garlic and 2 cups of the wine in a bowl. Put your Italian breadcrumbs in another bowl. Take each quarter, remove skin (if desired) and dip it in the wine mixture. Roll each piece in the breadcrumbs. Put the quarters in a roasting pan—stand them on their side, and fill the pan up with their little legs sticking up in the air. You can get many, many pieces of chicken in a roasting pan with this method. It also ensures that each piece of chicken will be well done. When the pan is full, pour 1 cup of white wine into the bottom of the pan. Place pan in oven and cook for approximately 2 hours at 350°F. Check the pan often, and add more wine as it is absorbed into the chicken. Add the wine to the bottom of the pan; don't pour it over the chicken. To check for doneness, stick a fork in the thigh part of a piece of chicken. If it goes in easily, the meat is done. Allow it to cook for an extra 15 minutes at this point to ensure that all the chicken is well done.

If you are cooking a large amount of chicken, place the cooked chicken in coolers to keep it warm. Line the cooler with a large garbage bag first; it will make cleaning much easier.

Figure 8 ounces of chicken per person. Serve leftover wine to your kitchen staff; they will need it.

GRILLED CHICKEN

Same ingredients as above except for the breadcrumbs

Mix the salt, pepper and garlic in a bowl. Add 3 cups of wine. Take each quarter, remove skin if desired, and dip it in the wine mixture. Place the chicken on the grill. Constantly baste the chicken with the wine mixture. Stir up more basting mixture, as you need it. Turn each piece of chicken regularly to ensure it cooks all the way through. To check for doneness, stick a fork in the thigh part of a piece of chicken. If it goes in easily, the meat is done. Figure 8 ounces per person.

PORK ROAST

10 pound pork roast
1 box whole cloves
cheap white wine
1 tablespoon salt
½ tablespoon pepper
¼ teaspoon cinnamon
¼ teaspoon nutmeg

Stick the cloves into the pork roast. (Don't go crazy with this and make it look like a porcupine. Clove numbs the tongue, and if you use too much, your taste buds will all go to sleep.) Space the cloves several inches apart. Mix the salt, pepper, cinnamon, nutmeg and wine in a bowl. Pour the mixture over the roast, and place it in oven at 350°F and let it cook for approx. 3.5 hours or until the internal temp. reaches 140°F. Baste the roast every 15 minutes or so using a brush or a turkey baster. When the roast is done, allow it to cool for about 15 minutes. Slice and serve. Pour the leftover pan drippings over the meat right before you serve. Figure 6 ounces per person.

You can make gravy with this, if you desire, by adding 2 tablespoons of breadcrumbs to the drippings and bringing that to a boil, reduce the heat and stir until the mixture thickens.

ROAST BEEF

10 pound beef roast
1 box cheap red wine
½ tablespoon salt
½ tablespoon pepper
½ tablespoon cinnamon
½ tablespoon nutmeg
½ tablespoon dry mustard

Poke holes in the roast with a long sharp knife. Place roast in roasting pan. Mix the wine, salt, pepper, cinnamon, nutmeg and dry mustard in a bowl. Pour mixture over roast. Place in oven and cook for approx 3.5 hours until the internal temp. reaches between 140°F for rare to 170°F for well done. Baste the meat every 15 minutes using a brush or a turkey baster. Mix more of the basting mixture if necessary. When roast is done, allow it to cool for approx. 15 minutes before you slice. Pour the pan drippings over the meat before you serve.

Figure 6 ounces per person.

POTATO SOUP

The easy way to do this is as follows:
1 package of potato soup mix that makes a gallon
1 gallon of milk
1 package cheddar cheese dip mix
1 pound raw potatoes for each package of soup mix
salt to taste, optional

Cook potatoes separately. Mix ingredients for soup mix in pot and place on low temp. This is a soup that will stick if you use aluminum pans, so I recommend a slow-cooker. Mix the cheese dip with enough milk to make it the consistency of a milk shake and stir it into the soup. When potatoes are soft, drain the water and add the potatoes to the soup mix. This makes a thick soup, almost a stew really. It will certainly stick to the ribs. Figure an 8-ounce serving per person, and make soup accordingly.

CHICKEN & RICE SOUP

1 pound of chicken per gallon of soup—off the bone weight
1 teaspoon salt
1 teaspoon pepper
1 box quick-cooking rice
1 stick butter
1 lemon
½ cup milk
1 package chicken bouillon cubes

Skin chicken (or not, as you prefer), salt and pepper each piece, place in a shallow dish and bake at 350°F until done. Remove chicken and allow to cool. Debone chicken and set aside. If you are making a gallon of soup, you need about a gallon of liquid, so measure the drippings from the chicken and pour that into the cook pot. Use chicken bouillon cubes dissolved in hot water to make up the difference in the liquid. Pour that into the pot and bring the ingredients to a boil. Turn down the heat and add more salt and pepper (if necessary), butter, lemon juice, milk, rice and chicken. Allow it to cook on low heat until the rice is tender. You may have to make more bouillon and add it in to make it more soupy.

Figure an 8-ounce serving per person.

A side note here: don't use a pot that only holds a gallon, you will have a fine mess on your hands as you add the chicken and the rice to this dish.

You can make this soup using canned chicken, but it is not as tasty.

ROSE PUDDING

First decide how much you want to make, and then get enough large boxes of vanilla pudding to do the job. We will use the measurements for one large family package; if you make more, remember to taste it as you add spices. You don't just double the amount.

1 large family package vanilla pudding
milk, according to package directions
2 tablespoons sugar
1 teaspoon cinnamon
1 teaspoon nutmeg
1 tablespoon vanilla extract
1 rose for each cup of milk

Take your roses and remove the petals, wash them with cold running water and place them on paper towels to dry. Put the milk, sugar, cinnamon, nutmeg and vanilla extract in a blender. Blend until all ingredients are mixed well. Pat the rose petals dry and add them to the blender. Puree this until you can no longer see any rose petals. Pour this mixture immediately into a large bowl and add the vanilla pudding. Mix with an electric mixer until the pudding becomes semi-firm and will not drip off the blades. Place bowl in fridge and let it gel for several hours—overnight is better. To serve, spoon it into dishes and garnish with a bit of cinnamon.

You can use your choice of roses for this dessert, red or white or yellow. Each color gives the dish a different flavor. I prefer white myself. Make several kinds and decide for yourself. No one in your house will complain about having to taste several different kinds of pudding.

You have to have a kitchen to make this dish on site, but you can make it ahead and transport it to your site. Spoon the mixture into large zipper-type freezer bags and place them in an ice chest with ice under them and over them. Keep the pudding iced down until you serve it.

This is a modern remix of a fifteenth century recipe. I tried it the old fashioned way. It takes too much time and it scorches and then you have to start over. My method is fast, sure, and people will beg for more.

TEA

In the South, tea is very important. In fact it is referred to as the "House Wine of the South." I make mine very sweet; I did not know there was any other way to make it. I add sugar until the sweetness makes my teeth itch, and then I add a cup more. You may sweeten to taste.

Tea is cheap, and it goes with any kind of food that you find yourself serving. Use the big family-size tea bags; each one makes a gallon of tea. Bring your water to a boil, and toss in the tea bags. Let it steep for about 7 minutes. Any less and your tea will be too weak; any longer and it will be bitter. No amount of sugar will fix that. But if it does happen, try adding a bit more boiling water and a pinch of salt. Add sugar to taste—if you have never made iced tea in large quantities; it will take more than you think. Remember it is supposed to be sweet. Taste it; you cannot make good tea without tasting it. When you have the mixture right, pour it into a dispenser while it is still hot. Set out ice, and let folks fill their cups with it and pour the tea over the ice. You should also make an unsweetened ice tea—I don't understand it, but I do it nonetheless. We use an insulated 5-gallon dispenser for the sweet tea, and we use a 2.5 gallon dispenser for the unsweetened tea. And we refill them a lot. Keep the water on the boil if you have a lot of dinner guests.

We also keep a full dispenser of both sweet tea and unsweetened tea available all day long. People get thirsty and need to quench their thirsts. You might want to put someone in charge of tea.

If you do not have a kitchen, use instant tea. It is unnatural, but it will do in a pinch.

ಆFriends, Neighborsಭ
ಆand the Mediaಭ
Oh, my!

First and foremost, when you are looking for a site for your festival, be up front with who you are. The first year of PUF, I was not really straight with the folks who ran the city park that we used because I was afraid of stirring up a hornet's nest. I told them that we were a group of folks who wanted to use the park for workshops, dinner and a bonfire.

The second year of PUF, I gave them the same story. That year we discovered the joys of the Internet, and we used it to advertise our festival. It worked great, and it was almost our undoing. About two weeks before the festival, I received a phone call from the park folks, and they were a bit upset. They told me that someone had called them, anonymously of course, and told them that *Witches* were using their park. Furthermore, the informant told them that the details of the event was all over the net, and due to that fact alone, the entire town would be over run with *Witches*. That created quite a stir in a small Southern town, I can tell you. I was actually worried that the park manager was going to pull our permit. So, I made an appointment to go down to the office and talk to the park people and see if we could work things out. We talked for about two hours before I convinced them that we were harmless. I reminded them that we had used the park the year before and nothing terrible had happened. We even cleaned up after ourselves, hauled away all of our trash and left the place better than we had found it. Finally they agreed that we could use the park, but it was a reluctant agreement. They were not happy with the decision. I think they only allowed us to use the park because they were worried about a lawsuit. I did not care why they agreed, only that they did. We pushed on, but from that point on, I kept looking over my shoulder. It made for an uncomfortable situation.

On the day of the festival, a woman drove through the gate and did not stop. She looked straight ahead as she drove by, and her jaw was set. She was a very unhappy woman. A few minutes later she drove back out, and she still did not look at us. We scratched our heads and wondered who she was. About ten minutes later, the local cops showed up. They smiled and waved as they drove in, and we smiled and waved back. Yes, you can say "HOLY SHIT" around a smile. They drove through the site and did not see children being eaten or cats being tortured, and they left again smiling and waving. I breathed a sigh of relief. I was glad that I had talked to the park officials, and we had all of our cards on the table.

We use a different park now and have been using it for about seven years; everyone is happy with the arrangement. It is not perfect, but it is good. We were up front with the park officials in the beginning. We explained to them that we were having a Pagan event; there would be workshops, merchants, drumming and whatnot. They were nervous the first year, but when we did not sacrifice cats, steal the children of other campers or cause any other problems, they felt better about us.

Over the years there have been some bumps in the road. One year someone called the local police to complain about the drumming. They came up with a ranger in tow and shut down the drum circle—early. The next day I went to the park officials to discuss this problem. I calmly asked what time the noise curfew went into effect in the park and was told that the noise curfew was 10:00 P.M. I told them that our drumming was shut down at 8:30 P.M. They promised that they would fix it, and they did. We did not have any more complaints about noise. We did our own part to fix the problem as well. We moved the drum circle to the back of the property where the land makes a small bowl. That really helped to muffle the sound. No more rangers or police officers have showed up to complain about the noise since we made the move.

One year at our present site, there were new rangers on duty, and they clearly did not like us. They came through the camp every hour or so and glared at us. Finally one of the rangers tracked me down and told me that we did not have the proper permits to allow vendors and that he intended to shut down our merchant row. That would have been a disaster. So, I went to the ranger in charge and told him the situation. The final decision was not his, but he promised to help us out. I reminded him what good tenants we had been. I did not hear any more that weekend, and we went about our business. But on Monday, I called the park commissioner and told him my tale. He was surprised to hear that someone thought we needed special permits for the merchants. He confirmed with me that the event was a private one and that we took reservations. He promised he would take care of the problem. He took care of the problem so well that we have never seen any of the rangers who hassled us again.

At this point in our relationship with the park folks, things are good. They like us and say they actually look forward to having us come out. We want them to like us. They have to rent to us, but they could make our stay very uncomfortable if they choose to do so. So we give them a win-win situation. We give them money, no trouble; and the place is in better shape when we leave. In turn they are nice to us. Everyone is happy with the arrangement.

When you find a site that is perfect for you, tell the folks you are dealing with the straight story. If they don't know what Pagans are, educate them. If it is a public property, they have to rent to you, but better if they understand you from the beginning. If you run into problems on the site, go to them with any problems that arise. Be calm and cool when you talk to them; don't walk in with a chip on your shoulder. Folks have a tendency to respond in kind. If you are calm and rational, odds are they will be as well. Don't go in spoiling for a fight because you will surely get one. You may even lose your site. Line out the facts and discuss the problem rationally, and you will be fine. Depending on the situation, you may have to do lots of deep breathing exercises to maintain your calm. It will be worth it if you can create a relationship with the people from whom you are renting. It will also create goodwill in the general community, and that is something that we Pagans need. That is just a fact of life. So do your best to make a good impression.

⋐Big Party⋑
The drums, the drums, the drums!

In order to have a really great festival, you need to put yourself in the mindset that your festival is a big party. True, you will have guests there that you don't really know; there might even be folks there that you don't like. And there will be classes and rituals. But really, it is just a party and you are the host. Think about how you treat people who come to your house to socialize. You greet them warmly and make them feel welcome. You feed them good stuff to eat, and you provide some sort of entertainment. You need to do the same thing with the folks who attend your festival.

This is not as hard as you may think. Treat the folks who come to your festival just like you treat the folks who come to your house for a party. Smile, be welcoming, let them know you are happy to see them, tell them what is happening and give them directions to the food and the bathroom. Make sure they don't fall in the fire, and help them to bed if they need it. See, just like at home.

Be available to your guests. Don't be too busy if someone needs to talk to you. Everyone needs to feel that they are important in the overall scheme of things. You owe it to your guests to give them some time if they want to have a conversation with you. A five-minute tête-à-tête with someone is not going to throw your entire schedule off track. Your guests will remember your kindness, and they will appreciate it.

I understand that your argument is, five minutes times 200 or 300 hundred people adds up. Yep, it does. But that is your job. Even if you are flying across the site to get from one disaster to another, you can at least smile and wave as you blow by.

Take time during meals to go from table to table, and ask folks how they are doing, find out if they are having a good time and see if they have any suggestions. Make sure no one is eating alone. If someone looks unhappy or uncomfortable, go over and find out what the problem might be. If it is a festival problem, listen and try to fix it. If your unhappy person had a fight with his or her significant other, give them a shoulder to cry on.

Now, take it a step further and get your entire staff in the same mindset. This has to be done well in advance of the festival, so they know what is expected of them. Make sure they understand that they are the hosts for a big party. Have them circulate among the guests doing the "ole grip-n-grin." Have them seek out folks who are at the festival alone, drag those folks over and introduce them to other folks. Have them think about the things they need to do to make folks feel more comfortable. This is why you need friendly folks on your staff.

Put someone personable on the front gate that will greet people with a friendly smile and let them know they are welcome and that you and your staff are happy to see them. This is especially necessary for the folks who venture out to festival alone. Remember that you set the tone for the festival, and your staff will do as you do. If you are the happy host, they will be happy as well. Most importantly, remember, shit runs downhill. If you are difficult, bossy and bad-tempered, your staff will be too, and that will make for an unhappy experience for everyone.

Go that extra mile for your folks. Make sure that things run on time, that there are a lot of activities, that everyone makes new friends, that everyone mingles and that everyone goes home with new information and a happy experience.

Just think of your festival as the biggest party that you throw all year long. Make sure that everyone has fun. That is your real job, host. I know you will be tired, sweaty, sunburned and sleep-deprived, but do it anyway. You will make or break your festival on how you treat your folks. The spotlight is on you, baby, because you are the big enchilada. This is your party, and with a lot of effort you can do it well. Paste that Vaseline-coated beauty-contestant smile on your face and hit the ground running. You can cry because your feet hurt in the privacy of your own bed at night.

As with any good party, things will go wrong. I have thrown parties where relationships broke up, people got together, illicit sex was had and babies were conceived. And those were just parties at my house. Think about this on a large scale. You will spend a good deal of time putting out fires. Do it quietly, behind the scenes, and with stealth. If disaster strikes, the whole world does not need to know about it. Find it and fix it. Don't run around like your hair is on fire—it makes folks nervous. And as the old TV commercial says, never let them see you sweat.

If you go into your festival feeling put upon and stressed and acting as if the entire thing is some kind of a huge burden and you are only doing this for the good of the *Community*, it won't be pretty. If you act like some sort of dictator who is constantly barking at folks and you allow your staff to act the same, folks will not come back. If you act like the martyr who is stooping to serve and wander around with a frown on your face, no one is going to have any fun, and that includes you.

So, your motto is more than *mi casa, su casa*. It is a Southern thing—"Come on in, kick your shoes off, tuck into some grub and let's party." Remember, if you act like the host of the party and encourage your staff to act the same way, your festival folk will be happy. And that is important. Because without them, what do you have? A big empty site and lots of bills that you can't pay.

ᴄ₃Program₈₀
Opportunity for cute cartoons

We use a program at PUF. It includes all of the pertinent information that anyone could possibly need. And probably a lot they don't. It tells where everything is such as the chow hall, the bathrooms, the cabins, the ritual fields, etc. It states the rules in black and white, gives bios of the workshop facilitators, the info on the workshops and also tells the mascot of the year story.

We sell ads in our programs; it helps to defray the printing cost. If you decide to sell ad space, go to your festival merchants first, then to Pagan-owned and Pagan-friendly businesses and pitch them. Remind them that the folks who come to your festival will have the document in hand all weekend long, and they will see the ad. It is a captive audience. Plus, many folks hang on to their program as a memento of the event. Make the ad space cheap so that anyone can afford to advertise.

We have a computer genius that sets up our program. I hope that you are lucky enough to have one as well. But if not, you can fiddle with it yourself, and eventually you will create a document that will make you happy. I say that in the belief that almost anyone out there is better with a computer than I am. Good luck.

After the program is created, call around to the printers in your area and get prices. You will be amazed at the difference you will find from printer to printer. This is also something that you should do every year because things change. Some years we get a better deal with a locally owned print shop (my favorite, because I believe in shopping locally), but some years we get a better price from one of the big printing chains. I hate that, but I have to keep the costs down—that is my job. So shop around for the best price in your area.

I have included portions of our program from a few years back. The layout was meant to be folded in half like a book. We put the map of the site in the middle of the program so that it folds out, and you can see the entire map. You are welcome to use our program as a guide.

PUF 2003

how the Penguins Came to PUF

Penguin: practically synonymous with gentle, friendly, enthusiastic, even goofy. An animal you might expect to see hanging around with Bill the Cat or dancing feverishly with Dick Van Dyke. These humanized images are, in fact, quite far from the truth. The average penguin is more likely to suffer from chronic depression, or at least chronic grouchiness. His toes are always cold, his wings completely useless (except in the water and that's cold too!) and he only sees the sun for about four months a year (and then it's up ALL the time and he can't sleep). Get the point?

About a year ago there was a particularly grouchy group (flock? gaggle? glob? See – they don't have a good *word* either!!) of penguins, who decided that everyone should be as miserable as they were. They organized the United Federation of Penguins, which quickly became notorious for seal-tipping, poking polar bears with spoons, carving rude statues out of the ice and other unusual Antarctic Antics.

Earning no respect on the Polar Cap, the Penguin Mafia decided to

PUF 2003

- Clothing is NOT optional. Please keep your clothes on at all times- This is a family event being held on state property and nudity is not allowed! Two-way radios are for use by staff ONLY! Anyone found to be tying up the channels for personal use will be asked to turn their radios over for the duration of the event.

- Drugs, alcohol, pets and firearms will not be tolerated
- ID Bracelets must be worn and visible at all times
- Trash containers are provided throughout the site, please use them!
- There is a recycling center outside the main hall, please use it!
- For the smokers-Butt cans have been provided around the site, please use them. Do not dispose of your cigarettes on the ground!
- Children MUST be accompanied by a parent at ALL TIMES!
- The kitchen is off limits to everyone except kitchen staff. No exceptions will be made!
- If, at any time, you require assistance from emergency personnel, (police, fire/rescue, towtrucks) please notify a staff member immediately.
- Please leave personal disagreements off the site. Fighting will not be

PUF 2003

Rituals

Libations to Inanna (Friday Evening Ritual)

Once upon a time, when the world was a little younger, there was a land watered by two great rivers and blessed by the Gods and nature. Inanna was the Goddess of that land and her people thrived and created many wonderful things. Today great armies of determined young men battle across that blessed land and great horror and destruction covers it. The Tigris and Euphrates run with blood, again. War is destruction and death: it is also a cleansing and renewing.

In this ritual, Inanna will be invited, enthroned and presented with the gifts of food, water, light, incense and wine. The high priest will perform this ritual in Sumerian and the high priestess will repeat it in English. At the culmination of the ritual, libations of beer and, water and love will be poured by all participants. All then will join in music and dance to honor her. It is a simple,

PUF 2003

Thursday Schedule of Events

3pm	Merchants Row Opens	Town Square
5pm	Dinner & Tavern	Prancing Penguin Tavern
7:15	Opening Ritual	Ritual Field
8pm	Laura Powers	Prancing Penguin Tavern

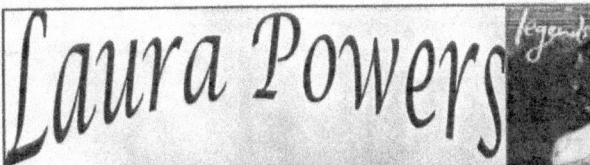

"Legends of the Goddess is enchanting and magical. Laura Powers is poetic and has the

PUF 2003

Friday Schedule of Events

7:30am	Breakfast	Prancing Penguin Tavern
	Morning Mantra	Ritual Field
8am	Gate Opens	
9am	Class Block I	Location:
	On Dying Presented by Ashleen O'Gaea	Prancing Penguin Tavern
	Basic Astrology *CanTeen Recommends	Puffin Pavilion
	Forming Your Own Magickal Group	Tent
10:40	Class Block II	Location:
	So You Wanna Be An Author Presented by M.R. Sellars	Prancing Penguin Tavern
	Dynasty of Ishtar	Puffin Pavilion
	Golden Meditation	Tent
	Children's Activity Meet at Kid's Corner	
12:10pm	LUNCH	
12:50	Class Block III	Location:
	Ritual 101 *CanTeen Recommends	Prancing Penguin Tavern
	Ancient & Modern Druidism Presented by Isaac Bonewits	Puffin Pavilion
	Celtic Reconstructionism	Tent

PUF 2003

Saturday Schedule of Events

Time	Event	Location
7:30am	Breakfast	Prancing Penguin Tavern
	Morning Mantra	Ritual Field
8am	Gate Opens	
9am	Class Block I	Location:
	History of Paganism	Prancing Penguin Tavern
	Hexerei: An American Magickal Tradition	Puffin Pavilion
	Introduction to Chakras *CanTeen Recommends	Tent
10:40	Class Block II	Location:
	Author Talk with Grey Cat	Prancing Penguin Tavern
	Performing a Druidic Liturgy Presented by Isaac Bonewits	Puffin Pavilion
	History of Tarot	Tent
	Children's Activity Meet at Kid's Corner	
12:10pm	LUNCH	
12:50	Class Block III	Location:
	The Art of Mehndi *CanTeen Recommends	Prancing Penguin Tavern
	Raising Witches Presented by Ashleen O'Gaea	Puffin Pavilion
	Cold Process Soapmaking	Tent
	Children's Activity Meet at Kid's Corner	

PUF 2003
Sunday Schedule of Events

8am	Breakfast	Prancing Penguin Tav-
9am	Closing Ritual	Ritual Field
10am	Site Clearing	

Everyone is expected to help out with clearing and cleaning the site. Your campsite should be completely cleared and cleaned and your trash should be taken to the dumpster near the Tavern. Cabins must be swept, mopped and left as they were when you arrived. Cabins/Campsites will be inspected as you leave the site. Please be conscious of your area and make this process easier for everyone.

Noon	Site Closes	

The Dynasty of Ishtar: Sumerian/Akkadian Magick
By John Gonce
Introduction to the magick and religion of Ancient Mesopotamia, focusing mainly on the worship of Ishtar/ Inanna. **John Gonce** has formal education in Christian Theology, Biblical Textual Criticism, and History of the Ancient Near East. A Reiki Master and a Priest of Inanna, he also co-wrote *The Necranomicon Files*.

Discover the Art of Mehndi   by Andi Houston
Introduction to the practical, decorative, and magical uses of henna. Class members will be able to mix their own mehndi and experiment with their own designs, or use the designs in the handouts provided. ($2 donation encouraged.)
Andi Houston specializes in the history of henna craft from different cultures, and is partial to North African geometric designs. She leads a Celtic Reconstructionism discussion group in Nashville.

Forming Your Own Magickal Group   by Lark
A discussion of important issues to consider when forming a

Introduction to Roman Reconstruction Paganism
by Patrick Owen
This class will introduce you to the concepts of Numinism, Nova Roma, and the private household rites that formed the core of Roman paganism for almost 1,200 years.
Patrick D. Owen, called Uncle or Father, is a native Tennessean who holds a degree in history from Rhodes College. He is a citizen of Nova Roma, as well as a High Priest, brewer, tobacconist, and aspiring philosopher.

Your Opinion Counts!

As you attend workshops you will be handed comment cards. Please take the time to fill these out and let us know what you think. Your feedback will help us when planning for

Special Events at PUF

Town Square: A new direction for networking and meeting new people. The Town Square will house the vendors as well as a central meeting place for PUF Attendees. BYOC (Bring Your Own Chair) and gather about at the Town Square's center tent. Enjoy drumming, music and friendship while relaxing in the middle of all the action.

Pagans In Recovery: A discussion group for Pagans in recovery for various reasons. Including addiction and abusive behaviors and beyond. Join others on the road to wellness to share ideas about putting a Pagan twist on recovery programs that normally target mainstream religion.

CanTeen: A meeting of the minds for teens age 13-18. This is a chance for all of our teen attendees to gather in their own place for discussion and the chance to get to know each

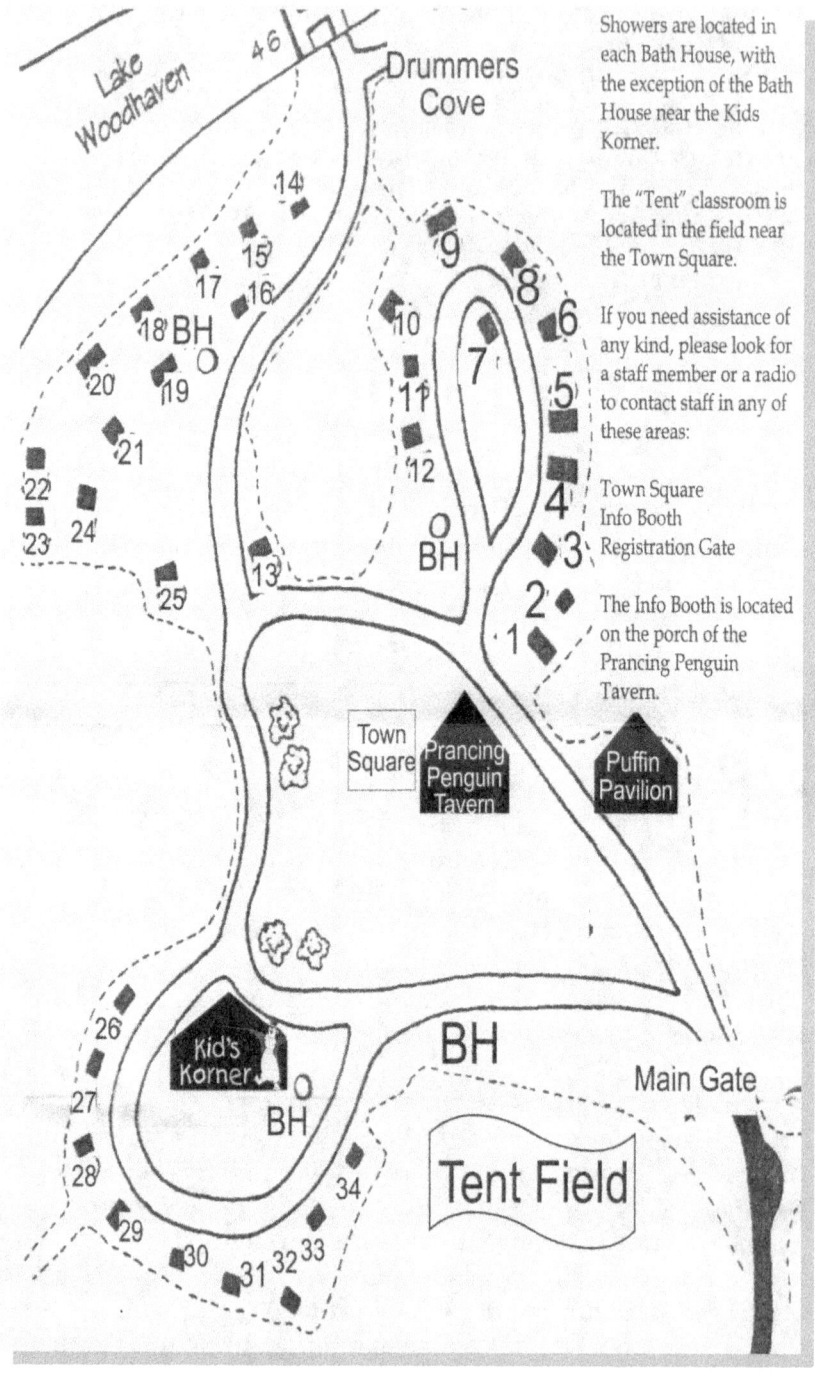

PUF 2003

Isaac Bonewits

Isaac Bonewits is one of North America's leading experts on ancient and modern Druidism, Witchcraft and the rapidly growing Earth Religions movement. A practicing Neopagan priest, scholar, teacher, bard and polytheologian for over thirty years, he has coined much of the vocabulary and articulated many of the issues that have shaped the rapidly growing Neopagan community in the United States and Canada, with opinions both playful and controversial.

As an author (of *Real Magic, Authentic Thaumaturgy*, and numerous articles, reviews and essays), a singer-songwriter (with three albums to his credit), and a "spellbinding" speaker, he has educated, enlightened and entertained two generations of modern Goddess worshippers, nature mystics, and followers of other minority belief systems, and has explained these movements to journalists, law enforcement

M.R. Sellars

Born February 20, 1962, M. R. Sellars began reading at age four, and writing shortly thereafter. He hasn't stopped since. The product of a liberal family, from an early age Sellars was exposed to many different religions and belief systems, both mainstream and obscure. To this day he remains an avid student of the religious diversity which surrounds us. Not one for remaining "in the broom closet," Sellars often gives group lectures on request in order to help dispel the many myths and misconceptions that surround the practice of WitchCraft and the Wiccan Religion.

An avid member of The Nature Conservancy and the World Wildlife Fund, Sellars resides in St. Louis with his wife and daughter. Locally, their home is known to be a haven for neglected and abused animals, and the ever changing population stands for the moment at one dog and nine cats.

Ashleen O'Gaea

Ashleen O'Gaea is the author of three (so far) books about Wicca. She's also a co-founder and Board member emerita of the 16-year-old Tucson Area Wiccan-Pagan Network, a co-founder, Board member, and senior Corresponding Priestess of Mother Earth Ministries-ATC, a Tucson-based neo-Pagan prison ministry; she's also the High Priestess of Campsight Coven and a co-founder and developer of Adventure Wicca. She's the bio-mommy of the now-grown Explorer, kitty-mommy of Bette Noire, Hal, and Milo, dog-mommy of Barleycorn, and life-long love and partner of Canyondancer.

Raising Witches

It takes a village to raise a Witch! Talking about "Raising Witches," O'Gaea explores the whys, whethers, and how-to's of community religious education for neo-Pagan children.

Grey Cat

A brief bio on Grey Cat's Craft experience in her own words:

"Somehow I'd missed all notice of the existence of modern Witchcraft all through the late 60s and the 70s, but somewhere around 1980 (you don't really want me to go upstairs and look up the date do you?) I got hold of a book called Drawing Down the Moon, by Margot Adler. Opened MY eyes! I fairly quickly got in touch with some Wiccans in the area and with the ones who became my teachers. I studied with Michael Ragan of the Temple of Danann for my first with a lot of help from Amber K. Seems like it was no time at all before I found myself with students of my own. My first class of five all made it to initiation and formed the nucleus of NorthWind. We have, it goes without saying, grown bigger, split, grown smaller, hived, added new students, lost

Laura Powers

"Legends of the Goddess" and "Beyond the Pale: Legends of the Goddess II" are the first and second cd in a three volume trilogy which feature musical themes based on the Celtic goddess. Powers' fascination and extensive research in Celtic mythology, combined with her talent as a singer/songwriter, led her to the creation of this project. The music, enhanced by instrumentation such as tin whistle, uilleann pipes and Irish flute melds with the lyrical imagery and her

Spiral Rhythm

Joining us to perform this year are Kerri Hirsch and Ric Neyer along with their group Spiral Rhythm. They come to us from Atlanta GA and have an extensive list of previous festival gigs. We are privileged and excited to have them here at PUF! You can check out their website at
www.spiralrhythm.com or
www.skyypilot.com

They will also be available in the Town Square area at their booth. They promise to have lots of interesting offerings there, and, will be offering impromptu drumming and performing throughout the days at PUF.

Midnight Madness in the Town Square

Join the Merchants of PUF for a Mid-

LET THE BURNINGS BEGIN

In February of 2001, serial killer Eldon Andrew Porter set about creating a modern day version of the 15th century inquisition and Witch trials. Following the tenets of the *Malleus Maleficarum* and his own insane interpretation of the Holy Bible, he tortured and subsequently murdered several innocent people.

During a showdown on the old Chain of Rocks Bridge, he narrowly escaped apprehension by the Greater St. Louis Major Case Squad.

In the process, his left arm was severely crippled by a gunshot fired at close range.

A gunshot fired by a man he was trying to kill.

A man who embraced the mystical arts.

A Witch.

Rowan Gant.

In December of that same year, Eldon Porter's fingerprints were found at the scene of

·☙·

Plan Your Classes Here!		PUF 2003
	Friday	
Time	Class	Location
9am-10:30		
10:40-12:10		
12:50-2:20		
2:30-4:00		

⚘Big-Nose Pagans⚘
Warts and all

We have been very fortunate over the years to have had some great guests at PUF. We started out with a couple of local folks as guest speakers, Tony Kail and Grey Cat. After a few years, word started getting out about our festival, and M. R. Sellars got in touch and asked if we would be interested in having him as a guest. He is a smart guy and was promoting himself by finding places where folks like me would let him set up shop and sell his wares to a captive audience. I went to his website, took a look, and I liked what I saw. He came, did great workshops and was a ball to party with too. He went home and wrote great things about us. Bless him. Because he has spoken so highly of us, other authors have been willing to take a chance on us and come do workshops too.

If you're not as lucky as we are to have your own private angel working on your side, there are a few things you can do to help yourself. Educate yourself; find out who is who in the Pagan world, who is writing what, how good they are, and whom the general audience that will be attending your festival favors. Damn, I sound like an owl. You have some favorite authors that you would really like a chance to meet; start your list of potential guests there. Do the legwork and find out who else does good work, and add them to your list. Go out and ask people in your community whom they are interested in seeing in the flesh, and add those names to your list. I even put this question out on several E-lists where I am a member and got lots of responses back. When your list of possible guest speakers is compiled, you may find that you know most of the names on it, and there may be a few you don't know.

This is where the research comes in to play. The names you are familiar with can get moved to the side for now. You need to find out about the other people. My best advice is to go to the net and do a Google search. Most of your potential guests will have their own websites, and you can check them out. If someone really peaks your interest, go and buy one of their books. Reading that will tell you all you need to know—maybe not all but at least enough for you to know if you want them to grace your festival or not.

After your research, it is time to make contact. Go back to the website, phone number, snail mail or whatever contact info you have for the person, and ask them how much they charge for a weekend festival. Also ask if they charge per workshop or just a flat fee. At this point, you may be priced out of the game. If so, thank them politely for their time and tell them that you cannot afford them yet. They will understand. If you are not priced out, give the author the dates for your festival, so they may check their availability. Do your research early; many of the Big-Nose Pagans are booking a year in advance. Some are booking even further in advance. You can't wait until three months from your festival and expect to be able to book a big name. Ain't gonna happen.

I realize that many people do not like to cold-call, but this is your job. BNP's expect people to contact them about festivals, and they will happily deal with you. After all, you are not trying to sell them burial plots, you are trying to help them make money. You may get some "no's" from a few of the folks you contact, and you may not even get a reply from some. Just keep slogging away at the list. And don't take rejection personally. It is just business.

Some authors now have PR people to handle their bookings, so don't be surprised to get a return email or phone call from someone you have never heard of before. The PR folks that I have dealt with have all been super, but remember that they have the best interest of their employer at heart, and they may be very firm with you on details and accommodations. Deal with the PR person as if you were dealing with the author, and you will get further in your negotiations.

There are a few other things you need to know before you nail down your BNP. Will they be bringing books to sell? Do they need any special accommodations? Are there special dietary concerns? Will they fly in? Will they drive? Will they be traveling alone? Are you responsible for their travel cost? That is usually a yes, unless they are driving over from the next town. If that is the case, you should at least offer them gas money.

Explain that in return for their services, you offer food, shelter, a place to sell books, travel fees and a whole lot of fun. If you have a website, send that address to them, so they can check you out.

At this point in the proceedings, you need to look at your money. If a BNP is costing you $500 in fees, and you have to fly him out of Zimbabwe, that is going to cost you extra. Take a look at ticket prices and add that into the cost. With the plane ticket fees included, your BNP may cost you $750 or more. Make sure that the budget can handle that amount. Again go to the net (how did we ever live without it?) and start looking at airline prices. Try one of the popular discount ticket websites first for bargain prices. Some companies will let you pay for a ticket in advance and will let you know if the price drops and will also give you the lower price. That is the bomb. It is a terrible feeling to buy a ticket for $250 and have that price drop by $50 or $60 and you miss out on the savings.

Sometimes a BNP will ask you to fly them at special times or get them home before midnight. That is only fair; they do have lives outside of your festival. You can play with ticket prices and time schedules and see if you can pull off their request. Sometimes a middle of the day flight will cost more, but a red-eye will be very cheap. We have brought Isaac Bonewits in for our festival for several years, and he lives two hours from the airport. With the new security precautions, he has to be there two hours before flight time. A red-eye will have him getting up at 3:00 A.M. But he has gamely done so because it allowed us to save money. Bless him.

There are a few wrinkles for you to iron out if your BNP is flying to your town. First, you will need to make sure that a member of your staff picks them up at the airport. You can't have them wandering around a strange country by themselves after all. Second, you might really want to bring a sign with his or her name on it, so your guest can find you. Not everyone looks like the picture on his or her book jacket, and you might not recognize them. This seems like a simple idea, but you would be surprised at how many festival organizers do not think of it. How they think their BNP is going to get to a festival site in a strange city is beyond me, but it happens. Don't let it happen to you.

If BNPs are flying into your festival and you are buying the tickets, there are several questions you want to ask. First, is the name on their book jacket the same name that is on their driver's license? You will have to book the ticket in the legal name. So ask, don't assume.

Sometimes a visiting BNP will want to rent a car because of other commitments in your area. Work out the details so that everyone knows what is expected of them.

Sometimes several groups will share the expense of a BNP. For example, an author may do a book signing at a shop, drive to the next town and do a workshop and then come to your festival. You get with the other folks that want the services of the BNP and work out the details. This arrangement can get hairy, but it can be worked out. Usually.

If the budget can stand all the costs involved, then you can firm up the deal with your chosen BNP. We do not have a standard contract with our BNP's; it is all done on a handshake. That works well for us and everyone is happy with the arrangement. They say they will come; we make the travel plans, check it out with them, bring them in, have a great weekend, pay them, feed them and send them home again. Some of the BNP's do have a contract for the festival to sign. They will tell you if that is the case. Don't get twitchy if this is the case with someone you contact. Just remember— this is business.

There are some authors who are willing to come to festivals and do workshops in return for food, a place to sleep and a place to sell their books. On a shoestring budget, these are the folks that you need to find. It is a win-win situation for everyone; you get an author, and they get a new market for their wares. Again, you have to go looking. We are not on a shoestring budget anymore (however, we do watch every penny), but I am always happy to get an author sans fee. It gives me more money to spend elsewhere.

Having authors at your event is a plus. It draws more guests to your festival, and that is good. It gives the locals an opportunity to meet the movers and shakers of the Pagan movement, and that is good too. You have the obligation to treat them well. Here's why: they are the elders of our community, and you should treat them as such. If that doesn't work for you, try this: they bring more people to your festival and that makes more money. If those two things are not enough to motivate you to treat your BNP's like royalty, I will give you one more. If you don't treat them well, they won't be back, and they will tell other BNP's about their experience. If that happens you will find yourself with no Big-Nose Pagans, and that will be very sad.

Do them right and they will do you right in return.
    Happy hunting!

BNP's w/ staffmember Beth
L. of Beth: M.R. Sellars & Isaac Bonewits
R. of Beth: Dorothy Morrison & Trish Telesco

Police Politics
How to handle the authorities

These are not really PUF stories, but I thought that I would include them in this book so that you can see some of the problems that might arise. We are still a minority in this country, and lots of people don't like us. Some fear us. That is a shame, and I hope that one day it will change, but for now this is the way things are.

For several years we used a state park for our Sabbat gatherings. We did not enlighten the park officials about the nature of the gatherings, but we had no trouble with them and thought we were ok.

After one of our small Sabbat gatherings, I discovered that even though we had been discreet, we had been knocked out of the broom closet. Seems that a high school kid in the local town where we met wrote a paper on Witches for his English class. Now it was supposed to be about the Witches in Mac Beth, but it ended up being about us. He wrote, "The witches in Mac Beth are like the ones that meet at the park. They light a white candle and a black candle, have a fancy dinner and then sell their souls to Satan." (This is a direct quote, no joke). We laughed about it, but the next time we tried to reserve the park, it was booked. It was booked every time after that. It became very *not* funny. I could not prove any discrimination, but I could not get a reservation either.

Another sobering event took place a few years after that. A large local group held regular gatherings for themselves on private land in the sticks. They were open and everyone was invited. They had several gatherings a year for several years and managed to keep under the local, fanatic, bible-banger radar. It was all good. Until one weekend when their luck ran out. The local law enforcement boys showed up with guns drawn and scared the hell out of all the Pagans present. Seems that they had received a complaint from a neighbor that there were a bunch of devil-worshipping-baby-killers in the woods. The cops hassled everyone and made some very ugly threats along the lines of "We'll just shoot ya all and let God sort ya out." They also threatened to turn all the children over to protective services, to confiscate everything on the property and so on and so forth.

Very ugly. The police set up a roadblock on the country road leading to the property where they stopped everyone and demanded to know what business they had in the area. The incident made the papers, of course. Someone else, who was not present for the proceedings, brought an accusation of animal sacrifice. She claimed ducks were sacrificed and then cooked and given to the participants, and her grandchildren became sick after eating the food that was served at the gathering. (This led to many duck and duck sauce jokes as you can imagine.) From all first hand accounts, the fried chicken served at that gathering was from the Colonel, which had already been sacrificed, rolled in batter and fried before ever getting on the site. No one was naked, and no babies were eaten. Sadly, despite the questionable behavior of the law enforcement officers up to and including probable 1st Amendment violations, that was the last gathering on that property. It was put on the market, and as far as I know, is still for sale.

Keep in mind that all this hoopla came from an anonymous phone call. The police did not check the situation out but came in with guns drawn. When they arrived on the scene, the most threatening sight that met their eyes was a bunch of folks eating dinner. At that point, they should have apologized and left, but instead they spent several hours terrorizing folks.

Sometimes even small gatherings can be threatened. I attended a handfasting in a local park. It was a park in which I had held circles both large and small for more than ten years and had never had a problem. But this was in October, and things have a tendency to get a little weird that time of year. The wedding party was small; there were only eight people present, including me. The groom had gone down to the park office and purchased a permit for the site. He told the woman who issued the permit that the purpose was a handfasting. In all the years that we have used the park, we have never hidden whom we were or what we were doing in the park. I myself have a very nice relationship with the woman in the park's reservations office.

The bride was young and nervous; she wore a beautiful white gown, flowers in her hair and fairy wings. The groom was handsome and nervous—tall and dressed in Renfaire clothes with a lovely cloak. A dear friend of mine performed the ceremony.

It was touching and wonderful. Everyone had tears in their eyes. As we were bringing down the circle and asking for blessings and protections on the park, six park rangers stormed the site. They roared into the area with searchlights on and jumped out of their cars with guns raised, cocked and loaded. Let me say here that if you have never had the pleasure of hearing a shotgun being cocked, it is an unmistakable and unforgettable sound. The park rangers screamed at us to freeze and raise our hands. Men with guns trained on us quickly surrounded us. They also had flashlights which they kept at our eye level and blinded us. They demanded to know where the other people were, and when we tried to answer, we were screamed at to answer when we were asked a question. Thus began an hour-long ordeal where we were searched, questioned and verbally abused, all while we had our hands raised and guns pointed at us. The permit for the site was produced within two minutes of the ranger's arrival, but that did not satisfy them. They asked us who we were, what we were doing and several more times, "Where are the other people."

We were accused of not shooting straight with the officers and telling only half-truths. I asked what those half-truths were and was told that I would not tell them my correct name. I had been asked what my name was, and the rangers wanted to argue with me. I told them that my name was Tish Owen, and my ID would show that to be the truth. We were accused of being unorthodox. Several of the rangers said, "If you didn't know what this was, and you came up on this, what would you think?" Another said "No matter what, you think that we are supposed to just walk up and make all nice with you people." We were asked what religion we were several times. One ranger asked if we were Wiccan. We explained that we were of several different faiths including Christian. One ranger, a man with whom I had had a long conversation about what we did in the park a year before this incident said, "This is a park, and you are trying to turn it into something else."

They continued to ask questions, and we did our best to answer. At one point a ranger told me that I was arguing with him, when all I was doing was trying to answer his questions. Another told me he did not like my attitude. I did not tell him that I was not real crazy about his either; it seemed the best idea at the time was to keep my smart opinions to myself. While this discussion was taking place, all the men in the party were searched. Finally, we were allowed to put our hands down. If you have never stood with your hands above your head for thirty minutes, let me tell you, it is not pleasant. If you have never stood with you hands above your head for thirty minutes while men have guns pointed at you, rest assured, it is really unpleasant. All through the ordeal, the bride cried, sometimes breaking into loud sobbing fits. They searched our belongings including all the ritual gear. They confiscated the sword and athame, after driving them both into a picnic table to prove they were sharp. They made us all produce IDs and took all our info and the tag numbers from our cars.

At least two of the rangers told the bride to stop crying because everything was just fine now, and there was no reason for her to continue crying. Which only made her cry harder and louder. Finally they left the immediate area and drove back down the road just barely out of sight. We began to clean up and make sure that we had gotten everything. We walked around the circle to make sure we had gotten all the tea lights. One of the rangers came running back to us and yelled, "What are you looking for?" We explained about the tea lights and once more the rangers retreated from the area. We loaded our cars and talked among ourselves, still in shock. One of the men chuckled and said, "Hey, this is the first shotgun handfasting ever." We all laughed, and that broke the tension. But not for long because our laughter brought the rangers storming back to ask what was going on, and one said, "We heard someone screaming!" We explained that someone had told a joke and that we were laughing. That did not seem to sit too well with them.

After a minute or two, another ranger approached us and demanded once again to know where all the rest of the people were, all the people who had run into the woods. We told him again, there was no one else. He then asked the same question and got the same answer. Then he told us to collect our stuff and get out of the park, despite the fact that it was one minute after 10:00 P.M., and the park does not close until 11:00 P.M. I make it a policy never to argue with men with guns, so we packed and drove down the gravel road heading for the paved road. But before we got to the main road, we were stopped, and our cars were checked one by one for a head count. They were still looking for the non-existent people who they were sure we had hidden in our cars. All in all it was a truly horrible night.

It does have a happy ending. I complained to the commissioner of the park in question and the city park commissioner. They were both fairly horrified about the incident. They set up a meeting where the grievances were discussed. We came to a good agreement—at least I think so. In the future, Pagans would make reservations and explain whom they were and what they would be doing. They would call the particular park, notify them and ask that the rangers on duty be notified. We would not take blades into the park. In return, the rangers would not hassle us.

We offered to present a workshop for the park rangers so that they would be educated about us. I did that workshop and it went well; intelligent questions were asked, and we had a good discussion. As of this writing, there have been no further problems with the rangers. In fact, when we have seen them while we were in the park, they have been polite and friendly. We usually invite them to have dinner with us.

I must add this note: on the first Sabbat that we celebrated in that park after the incident, the commissioner of the park dropped by. He was introduced, warmly welcomed and offered dinner. He is a very nice, very fair man—and brave too.

You might be wondering about the "extra people" that the rangers kept going on about. We wondered too and asked in the meeting. Seems that the ranger on duty that night smelled wood smoke and stopped to investigate. Now, the picnic area that we used had a fireplace. It was October, and it seemed like a good idea to have a fire. Instead of driving up the road to investigate, he crawled through the brush. He saw a bunch of people in a circle, candles and a big sword and thought he had found some Satanists. As he lay there watching us, he heard movement in the bushes and was sure that it was someone trying to sneak up on him. All I can say is, it is a big park with over 1000 acres. There is lots of wildlife in it, and much of that wildlife is nocturnal. Or maybe it was fairies.

So I have a bit of advice in dealing with the authorities. First and foremost, do not lose your composure! Don't cop an attitude; they hate that and they have guns. Answer their questions as calmly and as thoroughly as you are possibly able to do. Do not make any sudden moves; this should go without saying, but I will say it anyway. Do not get between them and what they are looking at, such as your altar. Do not be silly enough to tell them not to touch your ritual gear. You may inform them that the items in question are sacred tools, and you would like for them to be handled appropriately. They may or may not. Do what you are told to do. You can complain later to someone higher up the chain of command, and you will be in good health to make those complaints. Try to remember that while you may be scared of them, they might be scared of you too. They may think that you are Satanists, and they may have watched one too many horror movies. Take deep cleansing breaths and be calm. Ask your gods to protect you. Ask for your mind to be calm so that you can deal with the situation intelligently.

It is my sincere belief that the more we interact with non-Pagans, and they see that we are normal folks just like them, the better. The less these kinds of incidents occur, the happier and safer we will all be.

I hope you never need my advice on this subject.

Volunteers
You want me to do what?

Volunteers—what would we do without them? I can tell you. We would work ourselves into the ground, nothing would be on time, dinner would be burned, and no one would know where all the children had gone. In short, we would not be able to pull off a festival without them. So, we invite them to sign up to donate 1.5 hours of "community service" time to our festival. Ok, maybe "invite" is too mild a word for it. I know that some would substitute the word "coerce," or "demand," or "strong-arm" in place of "invite." It is all in how you look at a thing, I always say. Anyway, some people do the volunteer time willingly and then ask how else they may help. In fact, I have to say that one of the most frequent things that is said to me at PUF is, "What can I do to help out?" That is beautiful. Very few people complain about being forced into involuntary servitude. When they do, we explain that we could not do it without them. If that does not work, we tell them that without our volunteers we would have to employ a much larger staff, and we would have to raise our very reasonable price—a lot. This usually works.

In order to use your volunteers where they will do the most good, I suggest that, long before you ever get to the festival site, you sit down with your schedule and block out how many volunteers you will need for each hour of your festival. You will need a few at breakfast, both to help and to clean up, a few more at lunch, many more at dinner. We also include all of the maintenance of the site on our volunteer list. We have volunteers to clean the bathrooms several times a day, restock the bathrooms with toilet paper, paper towels and soap; empty the trash from the kitchen and common areas; gather firewood; set out the tiki torches, fill them with fuel and light them in the evening; walk the site and pick up trash and cigarette butts (we don't find much).

We have quite a crowd at PUF, and we usually work out the schedule as follows:

Breakfast — Two volunteers to set up and keep the food coming along with most of the staff. Two volunteers to clean up after breakfast.

Lunch — Six volunteers (these are usually our teens) to make the sandwich ingredients, bag all the food in baggies, fill the lunch sacks and hand them out. Four volunteers to clean up.

Dinner — Eight volunteers per shift between 2 and 6 P.M. to get dinner cooked. Our staff mans the chow line. We have eight more volunteers to help with the clean up. For all the other jobs, we use two people per shift for each job that needs to be done.

We have extended our volunteer times to Sunday morning. If a few of our festival folk would rather play all weekend and actually work on Sunday, that is fine by me. We need all of the hands we can get to clean up and clear the site at a reasonable time.

We ask our parents to volunteer their 1.5 hours in the children's activities area. That gives the folks in charge several sets of extra hands. At present, we have a large enough attendance at PUF that we can afford to allow our parents to volunteer just with the kids. Of course, we do have some parents that would like a break from their offspring for the weekend. That works for us too; we just put them to work someplace else.

We exempt our merchants from volunteer work; they are mainly professionals, and festivals are their bread and butter. They don't come to play but to make money. Plus, we charge for merchant space, and we con…I mean, we ask them to donate items for our raffle. We feel that they give enough to the festival.

We also exempt pregnant women and folks with special needs. That is not to say that they cannot volunteer if they want to. That has happened in the past; and we have happily taken them into service. We find a place for them where they can sit and help out; this is usually the front gate, the info booth or chopping veggies in the kitchen. Believe me, we never turn down help.

Before you get all guilty (Pagans do not do guilt) about asking people to pay for the weekend, bring food and work too, let me do the math for you. Most Pagan festivals are very reasonable in price (read "cheap"). Without asking your festival folk to kick in food and time, you would have to raise your prices. That might shut a lot of people out of the market.

How do you get them to actually show up for their work shift? We catch them at the front gate as they sign in; we show them the schedule of classes and ask them to pick a time to work. They look over the schedule and decide which class they can live without attending and sign up for their shift during that class block. The list of names is given to the person working the info booth. That person is in communication with all the staff members and can adjust where to send the volunteers at any given time block. Sometimes we have eight people assigned to the kitchen, and we decide we need ten. The volunteers are told to go to the info booth at their assigned work time to find out where they are needed. The person working the info booth checks off the names of the people who show up. Last but not least, that person sends me the names of the people who do not show up for their work assignment. I hunt them down. That is usually how we get the people needed to clean up after feast. It is the least favorite job at festival. We don't have much of a problem with no-shows.

Even doing community service can be fun. Many people who come to festival together will sign up for their volunteer shift at the same time and work together. They still get to hang out and still contribute to the general welfare of the festival. Another added bonus of "community service" is that it throws people together who might not otherwise meet during the course of the weekend. It is an opportunity to make new friends.

You are offering a win-win situation to your guests. They get a fabulous weekend at a small cost, and you can keep that cost down with their help. Besides, with the extra help, you will not be crazy and exhausted by the time the weekend is over, and you might actually get to have some fun too.

Forms
KISS

This section contains the forms that we use at PUF. You are welcome to adjust them to your needs and use them.

Adult Waiver of Participation
Pagan Unity Festival _____ (insert year)

I_____ do hereby state that I wish to participate in activities sponsored by Pagan Unity Festival Inc. at the Pagan Unity Festival. I understand that Pagan Unity Festival Inc. makes no representations or claims as to the condition or safety of the land, structures or surroundings of the property on which the festival is held, whether or not owned, leased, operated or maintained by Pagan Unity Festival Inc.

I understand that all activities are voluntary and that I do not have to participate unless I choose to do so. I understand that Pagan Unity Festival Inc. does not provide any insurance coverage for my property. I understand that I am responsible for my safety, my own health care needs and the protection of my property.

In exchange for allowing me to participate in the activities of the weekend, I agree to release from liability, agree to indemnify and hold harmless Pagan Unity Festival Inc. and any Pagan Unity Festival Inc. agent, acting within the scope of their duties, for any injuries that may occur to my person or my property.

This release shall be binding on myself, successors in interest, or any person or persons who would attempt to sue on my behalf.
I UNDERSTAND THAT THIS IS A LEGAL DOCUMENT. I HAVE READ, UNDERSTAND AND AGREE WITH ALL OF THE STATEMENTS AND TERMS IN THIS DOCUMENT. I UNDERSTAND THAT THIS DOCUMENT IS COMPLETE UNTO ITSELF AND THAT ANY ORAL PROMISES OR REPRESENTATIONS MADE TO ME CONCERNING THIS DOCUMENT AND/OR THE TERMS CONTAINED HEREIN ARE NOT BINDING UPON PAGAN UNITY

FESTIVAL INC. OR THE AGENTS OF PAGAN UNITY FESTIVAL INC. I EXECUTE THIS DOCUMENT VOLUNTARILY AND WITH FULL KNOWLEDGE OF ALL THE MEANINGS CONTAINED HEREIN.

LEGAL NAME (Please Print)
_____

LEGAL NAME (Signature)
_____

Detail any special needs, food allergies or any other medical condition of which the organizers of the festival need to be made aware.

Minor Waiver of Participation
Pagan Unity Festival _____ (insert year)

I_____ do hereby state that I wish my child: _____ participate in activities sponsored by Pagan Unity Festival Inc at the Pagan Unity Festival. I understand that Pagan Unity Festival Inc. makes no representations or claims as to the condition or safety of the land, structures or surroundings of the property on which the festival is held whether or not owned, leased, operated or maintained by Pagan Unity Festival Inc.

I understand that all activities are voluntary and that my child does not have to participate unless I choose to allow him/her to do so. I understand that by my consent to allow my child to participate I voluntarily accept and assume the risk of injury to my child or damage to my child's property.

I understand that Pagan Unity Festival Inc. does not provide any insurance coverage for my child's property. I understand that I am responsible for my child's safety, his/her health care needs and the protection of his/her property.

In exchange for allowing my child to participate in the activities of the weekend, I agree to release from liability, agree to indemnify and hold harmless Pagan Unity Festival Inc and any Pagan Unity Festival Inc agent, acting within the scope of their duties for any injuries that may occur to my child or my child's property.

This release shall also certify that I am the parent or legal guardian of this child. This release shall be binding on myself, successors in interest, or any person or persons who would attempt to sue on my behalf.

I UNDERSTAND THAT THIS IS A LEGAL DOCUMENT. I HAVE READ, UNDERSTAND AND AGREE WITH ALL OF THE STATEMENTS AND TERMS IN THIS DOCUMENT. I UNDERSTAND THAT THIS DOCUMENT IS COMPLETE UNTO ITSELF AND THAT ANY ORAL PROMISES OR REPRESENTATIONS MADE TO ME CONCERNING THIS DOCUMENT AND/OR THE TERMS CONTAINED HEREIN ARE NOT BINDING UPON PAGAN UNITY FESTIVAL INC. OR THE AGENTS OF PAGAN UNITY FESTIVAL INC. I EXECUTE THIS DOCUMENT VOLUNTARILY AND WITH FULL KNOWLEDGE OF ALL THE MEANINGS CONTAINED HEREIN.

LEGAL NAME OF CHILD (Please Print)

LEGAL NAME OF PARENT OR GUARDIAN (Please Print)

LEGAL NAME OF PARENT OR GUARDIAN (Signature)

Detail any special needs, food allergies or any other medical condition of which the organizers of the festival need to be made aware.

Merchant Contract with Pagan Unity Festival

We are looking for a wide variety of Merchants to inhabit our Merchants' Row and Town Square area. Festival Attendees like to see new and different items each year, and we look forward to bringing them an exciting array of merchandise.

Due to our policy of non-competition, Merchants are accepted on a first-come/first-served basis. We only allow 15-20 merchants each year and these spaces fill very quickly. Merchant Fees are $50 per 10'x12' space. This fee is payable at the time you are approved, along with your camping and entry fees.

Upon approval you will have seventy-two hours to accept and make payment of all fees. If payment is not made, we reserve the right to replace your booth with another merchant. You may pay your festival fees at any time.

If you are interested in vending at PUF, please fill in the form below and submit it. You will have an answer back quickly. Thank you for your interest.

I wish to participate as a merchant at the Pagan Unity Festival. I understand that Pagan Unity Festival Inc. makes no representations or claims as to the condition or safety of the land, structures or surroundings of the property on which the festival is held whether or not owned, leased, operated or maintained by Pagan Unity Festival Inc.

I understand that Pagan Unity Festival Inc. does not provide any insurance coverage for my merchandise or personal property. I understand that I am responsible for my safety, my own health care needs and the protection of my merchandise and my personal property.

I understand that if I cancel my booth at the festival less than 30 days before the date of the festival, no refunds will be given.

I understand that the Merchant Coordinator will assign all booth spaces on a first come/first served basis, except in the case of medical necessities. I will notify the Merchant Coordinator if I have special needs due to medical disabilities when I return this contract.

I agree to the following stipulations as a merchant at the Pagan Unity Festival:

- To release from liability, agree to indemnify and hold harmless Pagan Unity Festival Inc and any Pagan Unity Festival Inc agent, acting within the scope of their duties for any injuries that may occur to my person, my merchandise or my property.
- To arrive at the site at 12:00 Noon or after on the first day of the festival, and not before. I understand that if I arrive before the designated time, I will be turned away at the gate and will have to wait.

- To clear the site by 1:00 P.M. on the last day of the festival. I understand that this means that all of my merchandise, personal property, tents, campers and cars will be off the property at the set time.
- To pay all fees, camping and vending upon approval of this contract within two weeks of that approval. I understand that if payment is not made within that time, no space will be held for me.
- To not sell alcohol, illegal substances or paraphernalia.
- To hold blameless the Pagan Unity Festival for any merchandise or property that is lost, stolen or damaged.
- To be responsible for my own booth setup, tear down, booth needs (chairs, tables, awnings or tents) and clean up of booth site.
- To have my trash out for last pick-up, or take it away myself.
- To keep my vending area clear and free of debris at all times.
- To only sell the items that have been approved in advance by the Merchant Coordinator. I understand that if I display any items not approved, I will be asked to remove those items and put them out of sight.
- To comply with all state, county and local ordinances or regulations.
- I further understand that if I do not abide by these requirements, I will not be allowed to vend at PUF in the future.

In exchange, Pagan Unity Festival agrees to the following stipulations:

- To have the Merchant Coordinator or their designee available from the time of arrival to the time of departure.
- To provide security for the gathering.
- To arrange for trash pickup from the merchant area daily, or more often as needed.
- To exempt active merchants from the mandatory 1.5 hours of community service.

The festival coordinators request each merchant to donate one item to be placed in the raffle that will be held on Saturday evening. The money raised from the raffle is donated to a worthy Pagan person or charity. This is not mandatory.

I understand that this contract shall be binding on myself, successors in interest, or any person or persons who would attempt to sue on my behalf.

I UNDERSTAND THAT THIS IS A LEGAL DOCUMENT. I HAVE READ, UNDERSTAND AND AGREE WITH ALL OF THE STATEMENTS AND TERMS IN THIS DOCUMENT. I UNDERSTAND THAT THIS DOCUMENT IS COMPLETE UNTO ITSELF AND THAT ANY ORAL PROMISES OR REPRESENTATIONS MADE TO ME CONCERNING THIS DOCUMENT AND/OR THE TERMS CONTAINED HEREIN ARE NOT BINDING UPON PAGAN UNITY FESTIVAL INC OR THE AGENTS OF PAGAN UNITY FESTIVAL INC. I EXECUTE THIS DOCUMENT VOLUNTARILY AND WITH FULL KNOWLEDGE OF ALL THE MEANINGS CONTAINED HEREIN.

Name (Mundane please)
_____
Business/Booth Name
_____
E-mail address
_____

Snail Mail Address
_____
_____

Phone Number
_____

Have you vended at PUF before? YES _____ NO _____

If YES, Which year(s) _____

Preference will be given to vendors available for the run of the event. Will you be at the event for the entire time? Yes _____ No _____

If no, what days are you available? _____

How many 10x12 spaces will you need? _____
(Please remember each booth you rent requires another booth fee.)

Will you be sleeping in the merchant area? Yes _____ No _____

If the answer is no, what accommodations do you require?
Tent _____ Cabin _____ Camper _____

For how many people? _____

Adults _____ Children _____

Please list the merchandise you intend to bring to PUF.
_____
_____
_____
_____
_____

You will be notified within two weeks if there is a space available for you at the festival. At that time we ask that you pay your fees. A space will be held for you when the fees are paid.

෨Rules෩
We don't need no stinkin' rules!

When you are dealing with a bunch of folks, many of whom don't know one another, you need rules. Sad, but true. The place that you are renting might have rules, and those have to be enforced as well if you ever want to use that place again. Once you have decided what kind of festival you want to have, then you can decide on what kind of rules you will need. It may seem a simple thing to you that people should not build campfires wherever they wish with no stone ring to protect the area or that they should pick up their own trash. It is simple, but do you want to spend your entire weekend telling people the same thing over and over again? Spell it out for them, and then there is no argument—or there should not be. If a thing is in writing, it is easier to enforce.

So with that said, take a look at our rules. They may seem a bit dictatorial and sort of anal-retentive, but hey, I gotta be me. People have actually asked me if I was a former Marine. The answer to that is "No." I had much harder taskmistresses, Catholic nuns. They make the Marines looks like a bunch of sissies. Use what you like, and toss the rest, add more or scrap the entire idea. Some of them are specific to the camp we use, but most of them are only common sense. Sadly, common sense is not so common, or we would not need the stinkin' rules.

- Clothing is not optional. Please keep your clothes on at all times. This is a family event being held on state property, and nudity is not allowed!
- Two-way radios are for use by staff only! Anyone found to be tying up the channels for personal use will be asked to turn their radios over for the duration of the event.
- Drugs will not be tolerated.

Rules

- Firearms, WMDs, drunken behavior, bad attitudes, violence or other inappropriate behavior will not be tolerated. We ain't kidding.
- ID Bracelets must be worn and visible at all times.
- Trash containers are provided throughout the site. Please use them!
- There is a recycling center outside the main hall. Please use it!
- Do not dispose of your cigarettes on the ground! Butt cans have been provided around the site. Please use them.
- Children are not to be left unattended at any time. Any found will be sold as slaves. There are activities for children ages 3 to 11. Older children may attend classes. There are activities for teens. Please remember that your children are your responsibility.
- The kitchen is off limits to everyone except kitchen staff and volunteers. No exceptions will be made! Violators will be cooked and eaten.
- Please leave personal disagreements off the site. Fighting, arguments or rude behavior will not be tolerated on site.
- No swimming in the lake. The high snapping turtle population takes all the fun out of it.
- You must work your 1-1/2 hours of volunteer time at the times designated to you at the gate. If you do not show up for your assigned work schedule, you will be hunted down and made to wash all of the dinner dishes by yourself! Plus, we will tell everyone you are a slacker!
- There are two designated fire pit areas. No other fires are allowed.
- When you enter the site, you will receive a large trash bag. At the end of your stay, place your garbage in the dumpster outside the main hall. If at any point you need another trash bag, please ask a staff member.
- You are responsible for cleaning your cabin and campsite before you leave. Please be considerate and leave the area in the condition it was when you arrived. Better would be better. Each cabin must be swept and mopped. Brooms, mops and cleaner are available in each bathhouse.
- After 10 P.M., no drumming except at the lakeside designated drumming area.

- After midnight, no singing, chanting or yelling.
- A parent or legal guardian must accompany all children, or the parent must provide a notarized permission slip.
- No pets. Service dogs only are permitted at this gathering site. All other pets will be refused at the gate, so please do not bring them.
- Should you be unable to attend the event after purchasing tickets, you may request a refund. Requests received at least 30 days prior to the event will be honored. Requests received after that cannot be honored. Refund checks will be mailed within 30 days after the end of the event.
- Violators of these rules are subject to removal from the site with no refund of their fees.
- We reserve the right to revise these policies without notice.

NOT REALLY RULES, JUST GOOD ETIQUETTE

- If there are small children nearby, you may want to consider the language you use. Many parents would prefer that curse words not be used around their young ones.
- Please do not "blast" your music. Others may not enjoy your music as much as you do.
- If the majority of the folks in your camp are ready to go to bed, please keep your voices down or move to one of the common areas. If you are the only one who is ready for sleep, don't expect everyone else to be quiet!
- If there is an altar in your campsite, please respect it. Do not set empty drink cans or cups on the altar. Never touch others' magickal tools (wands, amulets, chalices, etc.) without permission.
- If you are invited to visit in a campsite, please do not assume this gives you license to go into their cooler or food supply.
- Don't enter a tent, camper or cabin without permission!
- Bring enough food and drink for the weekend. Don't assume others will provide for you.
- Bring appropriate clothing/bedding for the weekend. Remember to bring wet and cold weather gear. Around here, the weather can change without much notice.

Rules

- Children are welcome at our event, but please make sure they are cared for. Do not assume that other folks will be willing to watch your children. Explain to your children that they must be with you at all times or in the children's activities area. Make sure they are aware of the location of the Kitchen, the First Aid station and Registration.
- Clean up after yourself at the showers and bathrooms. Remember, you are not the only person using these facilities. Even if your mother is here, she is not responsible for cleaning up after you.
- Clean up after yourself after meals; don't leave your plates and whatnot on the tables and expect someone else to pick them up. See "mother" disclaimer above.
- Please pick up any stray trash or cigarette butts you find lying on the ground. If you attend the Drum Circle (or any other fire or party), please do not leave your empties (soda, water or whatnot) behind. Pick them up and dispose of them properly when you leave the area.
- Be careful with your blades and staves. Don't wave them around in a crowd. You could put an eye out.
- Treat each other with respect and respect all paths.
- Bring a positive attitude.

Merchants

∽PUF Stories∾
Once upon a time...

Anytime you get a bunch of crazy Pagans together, funny stuff happens. I thought it might be a good idea to include some of the stories, so you will see that you are not the only ones that are crazy.

Flying Pigs! — We decided to roast pigs over an open pit the second year of PUF. Don't ask, I thought it was a good idea at the time. There were several people who had cooked pig in this manner before and volunteered to do the job. As I was a novice at cooking whole pigs over an open fire, I really had no idea how long it would take for them to get totally done. (Turned out that the cooking time varies.) So, we set about digging a pit early that morning, laid the fire and let it burn down into coals. As that was happening, the pigs arrived, delivered by a brave woman named DayStar. The farmer had dressed them, and they were ready for the fire. They were not big pigs, which I expected. But I was a little dismayed to see that they still had their heads attached. It made the whole experience a bit surreal. We placed the grates over the fire and added the pigs. The pigs roasted all day, and a marinade was added to them occasionally. After a few hours, the folks cooking the pigs began to look a little roasted too. But they hung in there. The delicious smell filled the woods and drew people to the fire pit to check on the progress.

If you have never cooked whole pigs over an open fire, know that as they cook the skin shrinks. The pigs began to look for all the world as if they were smiling. One little boy asked the fellow cooking why the pigs were smiling. His reply was, "Because they are so happy to be our dinner!" I don't know if the kid bought that line or not, but he walked away looking very thoughtful.

Dinner was a little late that year because you can't always plan on when a pig will be completely done when cooked over a fire. And of course, no one thought to bring a meat thermometer. Plus, you have to carve the meat off the bone, and that takes some time too. But nonetheless, people got fed, and after they tasted the meat, no one complained. And the inquisitive kid who asked about the smiling pigs had no trouble putting away his share of pig that evening, no questions asked.

After dinner, the evening was spent dodging pig heads. We removed the pig's heads after they were cooked. We did not dispose of the heads sufficiently enough, to our later dismay. Some folks, who thought they were comedians, confiscated the pig heads. They put them in odd places: car hoods, by the campfire with cigarettes in their mouths and cans of beer nearby, in the women's bathroom high on a ledge. And they were all still smiling. Did I mention that there was electricity only at the pavilion on that site? We used torches on the pathways and candles in the bathrooms. So the bathrooms were fairly dark and full of shadows. There is nothing to compare to a 3:00 A.M. trip to the potty, sitting down half asleep and glancing up to see a pig head on the stall wall grinning down at you. Priceless!

Far into the night, the country air was punctuated by screams and maniacal laughter. I threatened death to the miscreants if I woke up in the morning and found a pig head on the pillow next to me ala *The Godfather*. I am thankful to say that did not happen. But when we cleaned up the next day, we only found four pig heads, where there were originally five. We never did find the last one. I have bad moments when my fertile imagination runs away and gives me visions of a troop of boy scouts finding the hideous smiling thing.

Burning down the house! — The third year of PUF, we used a site that includes a new smoke house. The fee to use it was extra, and we felt that it was worth the money. On Friday afternoon, we gathered deadfall for the smoke house fire and got it started. A lot of wood, by the way. When the wood had burned down to embers, we threw the hot coals into the firebox and put the pigs and goats on the grill. Smoking takes a lot longer than grilling, and we wanted them ready for Saturday night dinner. Several people tended the fire and the meat during the evening and all through the next day. It was not as bad as standing over a fire pit, but it was still hot, sweaty work.

I went to bed that night content in the knowledge that all was in hand. The next morning I was on breakfast duty, so after that got underway, I went to check on the meat that had been smoking all night. Sometime during the four hours I slept, we had a fire in the smoke house. Now the idea is to build a fire, let it burn down to coals and then place the coals in the firebox under the grill and let the meat smoke. Hence the name "smoke house." Well, we had not considered that the pigs would drip grease, a lot of grease. And I have a suspicion that someone, trying to help, had actually put fire in the smoke house. The upshot was that the drippings started a real inferno, and unfortunately, the smoke house was not designed for that. The metal cover of the grill was warped, and the wooden handle (I know, I asked the same question, "Why would you use wood in a place were there is fire?") was charred completely away, and there were cracks in the concrete block foundation. One of the little piggies was sort of charred too. I almost had a heart attack when I found the disaster. Nothing like a huge adrenaline rush to get the day started—better than coffee. I rounded up some help, and we started all over again. We cleaned out the coals, built a new fire, let that burn down, placed them in the smoke house and then took turns watching those coals like hawks the rest of the day. But the damage was done, and I knew we would have to pay for it. The cost of doing business is sometimes high, but I did not look forward to explaining to the ranger how we set the smoke house on fire.

The ranger came up to look over the site on Sunday for check out. He was to see what damage was done over the weekend and see if the place was left clean. It was clean and there was also damage. I showed him the smoke house and tried to explain what had happened. He was really horrified; the smoke house was brand new. I told him that we would pay for the repair; he only had to let me know how much. He promised to get an estimate as soon as possible and call me with the amount. That done, I made reservations for the next year.

So on our fourth year, we made a little profit, and most of it went to repair the smoke house—over $300! Not to mention that we looked like idiots.

Burning down the house, part 2 — The next year, we decided we would have no pigs and no smoke house. We could not take the financial hit two years in a row. But here is the real story. I thought that we would live in infamy because of the fire. But that was not the case. When we checked in, the ranger asked us if we would be using the smoke house. We told him no. He then went on to regale us with the story of the group of people who had set the smoke house on fire the year before. We laughed in the right places and waved as he left. I could not decide if I was embarrassed or grateful that he did not know we were the arsonists. Some times the gods do smile on us.

It's the soap! It's the soap! — One year, Beth had volunteered to be the person in charge of the children. This gave our regular childcare person the year off. After several years in this job, Lynn deserved a vacation. Beth made her preparations on Friday morning to get ready for the onslaught of children. The cabin was well stocked with games, toys and books to keep the children occupied for the day. I was in the kitchen as she came through on her way to the bathroom. When she emerged a few minutes later, she reported that she did not feel well. She did not look well either. In fact she looked so unwell that I got on the radio and yelled for our EMT. As she slid down the wall to crumple on the floor, she said, "It's the soap, it's the soap." While that may sound like a cryptic message in a spy movie, I knew we were using handmade soap provided by one of our merchants. It was the same soap that I had sold in my shop for years. Never, never had anyone had a reaction to it. But reaction she was definitely having. She changed color on me, and her breathing became raspy. I yelled into the radio some more. I was quickly approaching a panic mode. I had not broadcast who was in need of help, and at that moment a member of staff inquired as to where Beth might be, as there were children arriving at the kid cabin, and there was no one in charge. I gave the only answer I could, "Beth is on the floor of the kitchen having an allergic reaction to the soap! Stay at the children's cabin until we can get someone up there. It won't be Beth." That created some bedlam on the radio; everyone was talking to everyone else. Finally, our EMT arrived. It seemed like it took hours, but really I know it was only a few minutes since I had put out the panic call. He took one look at her and confirmed the diagnosis. He gave her drugs, we sent for burly men to take her to her cabin and put her to bed. All the while, she kept trying to talk to me about what to do about the children. But she was dizzy, and her lips were swelling, and it came out sounding like "Mot abo dah chillen?" I tried not to laugh as I assured her that we would think of something. I watched as she was hauled away and shook my head. We had already had drama (Beth's) and hysteria (mine), and it was only 9:00 A.M. on Friday morning. As for Beth, she was mostly dead all day, but she got better. Actually, she rallied and managed to get to the kids by about 9:30. She is a champ!

The Viking funeral — We were in the middle of the main ritual, having a great time, when my friend Billy entered the circle, clapping in time to the chanting, and made his way over to me. He whispered in my ear, "Patrick has fallen, and I think he is hurt badly." Patrick is my husband. I clapped and danced my way over to DayStar and repeated Billy's message to her. She clapped and chanted her way out of the circle and headed for the location of the labyrinth where my injured husband was lying. I waited until the energy cone was fired and then slipped out of circle myself. At that point, no one in the ritual had any idea that anything was wrong.

By the time I got to the scene of the accident, Patrick has been lifted on to a massage table in the middle of the field, and lots of people were working on him. One of my daughters, who is a massage therapist, was there. There was also another massage therapist, lots of energy workers and a person who was trained in hypnosis. Someone had already put ice on his back to keep the swelling down. By using hypnosis, Patrick was put under, so he would not feel the pain, and so he would not move while we were working on him. According to my daughter (whom I must say here is one of the best healers I have ever worked with), he had at least five vertebrae out and a hip displaced. I started to sweat. He was massaged and had tons of energy pumped into him when finally my daughter started to put his vertebras back into place. She was sweating too, so I asked her why. She told me that one of the vertebrae was so far out of place that she was afraid that she would sever his spine by trying to put it back. I started to pray and called in every healing force I could name and asked that her hands be guided. She started with the least problem and went right up the spine. Everything slipped in to place like magick and as each one went into place her smile grew larger. Then she put the hip back into place. By then we were all sweating.

    About this time the ritual was ending, and so I slipped back in and made an announcement, which was, "I need six big strong men to come with me right now." I did not think about how it sounded, but it worked, and many big strong men followed me. I could hear the crowd behind me discussing what was happening, and finally they figured out that there had been an accident. Suddenly everyone in circle flowed across the field, and they all offered help. Someone went running for the torches that had ringed the ritual and called to others to help her. I looked around me and saw at least one hundred people standing there ready to help, their faces lined with concern. It was breathtaking. They did not know what had happened or who was hurt, but they did not care. They only wanted to help. We positioned men around the massage table and told them the object of the exercise was to take Patrick to the cabin across the field and not drop him along the way. The cabin had a large front room with good light and a fireplace for warmth. It was the perfect place to work on him some more. It was a long way to the cabin, so we told people when they got tired to sing out and someone would step in and replace them. We started off, and people got in front of us and beside us with torches to light the way. Others checked the ground in front, looking for holes that might trip us and guided us around them as we walked. I was told later that it looked like a Viking funeral procession going across the field with all the torch and lantern light and the body on the table.

    When we got to the cabin, we had to hand the table in since the door was too narrow to carry it through. Much sweating happened at that point, but we worked the table through the doorway with a minimum of shaking. Everyone on the site who had any healing ability followed us into the cabin. A fire was lit, and we took positions around him and began to work. My daughter directed our efforts. We worked for a long time, probably all told, two hours. All at once he startled us all when he woke up and shouted my name. We all jumped like rabbits. We had him move his arms and legs and wiggle his toes. We grilled him about how he felt. He asked us the usual questions, "What happened? Where am I?" We told him. He wanted to know how he had gotten from the field into the cabin, and we told him we carried him. "What! Are you all crazy? I must weigh at least three hundred pounds plus the table!"

At that point the tension was released, and we all laughed. My daughter was sick from the level of fear she had been dealing with, one woman was high as a kite because she was not accustomed to working with the amount of energy we had generated, and the rest of us were just wiped out. I decided he did not need to move to a bed and could rest quite well on the massage table in the common area of the cabin for the night. The healers in the room hugged each other, and we all were grinning and laughing. It had been an amazing experience, scary but amazing. Thirty people who for the most part used different healing methods, and many who had never worked together before, had come together in a dire emergency and flowed together so smoothly it was seamless.

Every time I tell this story, I get teary-eyed for a lot of different reasons. My husband was badly hurt, and I was scared. But what really gets to me whenever I think or talk about that night was the level of caring that I saw. Everyone at the festival stepped up to the plate to help. Every healer on site took part; people who did not heal carried Patrick across the field, gathered firewood, built the fire, carried drinks for the healers, and prayed to their gods that all would go well. When we were finally finished and I stepped outside for a breath of air, I found the yard full of people who were waiting for the outcome. They were just standing in the dark and silently waiting for news. I am still overwhelmed by the memory of love that flowed that night from friends and perfect strangers alike. We all pulled together with a common goal in our hearts and minds. That night I saw the best of what we are and what we do. It makes me proud and humble and joyful to be on this path.

As we sat in the cool evening and discussed the events of the night, we found that we had cause for amusement for several reasons. One was the description of Billy dancing into circle, clapping and singing, and DayStar and I leaving in the same manner. We laughed over that loud and long. Then someone else recounted my request for "large strong men" and congratulated me on the fact that quite several young men had followed me into the night. We decompressed with laughter and finally wound down enough to sleep. What a night—it will live in my heart forever. I will take this opportunity to thank everyone who was present that night, those of you whom I know and love and those of you whom I do not know. Bless you all.

 **And lo, the tomb was empty!** — This is a footnote to the proceeding story, and I had to include it here. There are actually two footnotes to this story. Some time in the wee hours of the morning, one of the security thugs heard a loud thump from inside the cabin and immediately thought that Patrick had fallen from the massage table. He rushed inside, scared about what he would find, only to find the bed empty and the sheet thrown aside. "Just like Easter morning!" His quote, not mine. He searched until he found the missing patient, who was just looking for the bathroom.

At breakfast time the next morning, I saw my husband ambling toward the bathhouse without so much as a limp. I was amazed that he was moving at all. He allowed as to how he was only as sore as if he had danced all night. Unbelievable! I talked to a friend of mine who is a paramedic about the incident. He told me what would have happened at the emergency room, and folks, it is not a pretty story. All told, I like our methods better. Nonetheless, I talked him into coming to PUF as our on-site paramedic.

Let me add one word of caution to my tale. We had a lot of good, trained healers that night, and even with the amount of talent we had, I think the gods were smiling on us as well. Please don't think that my story means you don't need a hospital in an emergency. We were lucky and blessed. Now, at PUF we have an EMT to tell us when we need to go to the hospital.

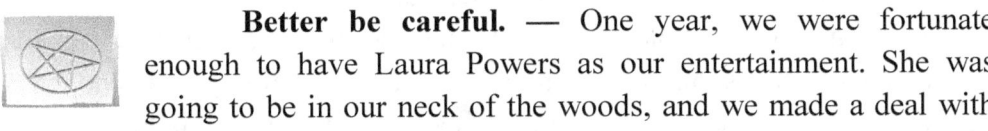 **Better be careful.** — One year, we were fortunate enough to have Laura Powers as our entertainment. She was going to be in our neck of the woods, and we made a deal with her. She flew into Nashville from California and sat with a nice young man during the entire trip. They engaged in the usual conversation; who are you, why are you going to Nashville and so on. He was returning to Nashville, his home, from a missionary trip, he explained. At which point he introduced her to some of his fellow missionaries. There were quite a few of them on the plane. He inquired as to her line of work, and she told him she was a singer. He asked if she would be singing in Nashville, and she told him she would actually be singing in Burns, TN. He got a strange look on his face and leaned over to whisper, "You should be very careful while you are in Burns. We understand that there is a Witch convention going on there." She

somehow managed to keep a straight face while assuring him that she would indeed be careful and be on the lookout for Witches during her stay.

The Governor! — It sometimes amazes me how information comes back to me. A friend of mine went to Iraq. He fell into conversation with some MPs from Nashville. In fact, they were on the Governor's security staff in the real world. They were regaling the troops with stories of the things they had seen and done in service of the great state of Tennessee. They told the story of how the Governor had sent them to Burns, TN to check out a bunch of Pagans who were using the state park there. You could have knocked me down with a feather. I never suspected we had been infiltrated. All I can figure is that they came to the gate, paid the admission price and checked out the site. I guess we passed muster.

A Witch, a Druid and a Goth girl walk into a bar... — Ok, so sometimes things get silly at a festival, for no apparent reason. One night, I was in the kitchen getting things set up for breakfast. Someone wandered in and starting helping me, and then several more folks sort of drifted in too. Someone told a bad joke, then someone else told another, then another. More folks showed up and they had jokes too. It became a non-stop joke marathon that lasted for more than an hour. Every one that came into the kitchen added their jokes, and it just kept on and on. We were laughing and holding our sides because it hurt so much. It was just one of those silly, spontaneous, middle of the night things that happen at festivals. Like the entire staff standing in a circle in the field talking to each other on the radios. Sleep deprivation can really screw you up.

Why are there animals? — We really have no good answers to that question, except that it amuses us. We did not start out with an animal or even a name. We started out with a one-day festival and just called it the local Pagan festival. Now that is a name that inspires.

The festival provided the food the first year, 'cause I did not know any better. That was the biggest expense. Since the first festival came out of my own pocket, which was pretty thin, I looked for ways to defray that cost. A friend of a friend worked at a bagel place that did not sell their day old bagels. They went into the trash. The manager was delighted to donate all the day old bagels to us since he felt bad about just throwing them away. So we picked up garbage bags full of bagels for three days before the festival—lots and lots of bagels. We stored them in my basement where it was cool, and they would keep. You know how it is when you have not had enough sleep and everything becomes funny? It was the same way with the bagels; they just became funny. For weeks after, someone would just say "bagel" and everyone would crack up. My car smelled of onion and blueberry bagels for weeks. I can tell you that is not a happy combination. We had bagels with cream cheese for breakfast, tuna and chicken salad on bagels for lunch, and bagels with everything else for dinner. We fed the kids and anyone else snacks of bagels.

We finally started to throw folks off site, so we could clean the place up. There was just one tiny problem; we ended up with so many bagels left over we could have fed a small hungry nation. I knew I could not stand to look at them in the cold, gray light of dawn. I knew I could not eat any more of them, maybe ever. We discussed building houses with them—or even a small town. Then we hit upon a brilliant idea! We pawned off as many of them as we could to our departing guests. I even resorted to threatening folks by telling them they could not leave unless they took some home with them. The wild creatures in the woods ate bagels too. So as you must know by now, the first Middle Tennessee Pagan festival was dubbed "Bagel Fest."

The second year of the festival, we were dubbed "Pig Fest." It was a moniker that we just had to live with. So I guess it was the weird chain of events from having pig for dinner to chasing each other with severed pigs heads that first brought an animal into the mix.

The third year of the festival someone dubbed us the Pagan Unity Festival and Lady Weaver designed a logo, a big red and green dragon. Because of the dragon, people started calling the festival...are you ready? Of course, you already know it....PUF, the magic festival. Although by Sunday of the festival, after the smoke house fire and my husband's accident, we had acquired two more nicknames, "Fire Island Festival" and the "Night of the Vertebrae." Because of course, both the smoke house disaster and my husband's disaster took place the same year. Luckily, only the name PUF seems to have stuck.

As for the rest of the animals that have joined us over the years, it really was mostly accidental. The fourth year we had sheep, for no good reason except that sheep are kinda funny, and we thought our dragon needed a little friend. We created a story that explained why the sheep were at PUF. We bought several hundred kushball sheep and hid them all over the site for the kids to find. We made cardboard sheep, gave them tomato stick legs and planted them all over the fields. We printed T-shirts that year, and we had our big beautiful dragon on it and one slightly singed and confused-looking sheep as well. That year we were "A Sheep's Oddesy." Before the festival was over though, many of our sheep began to disappear, and ransom notes were left in their empty places. The notes were all signed, "The Penguin Mafia." It takes almost no imagination to figure out what happened next.

The fifth year, the Penguin Mafia took over. We had another story about the cute little guys just looking for a place to be warm. We had a dozen or so little hard foam penguins, and we set them up on the mantle in the chow hall. They were cute and brightened the place up, so we left them there and went about our business. Then without warning, one of the penguins disappeared. Hard on the heels of the disappearance, a ransom note appeared. It did not make a lot of sense—there were threats made against the life of the hostage penguin and a demand for more fish at meals. It was written badly and signed by a polar bear. They don't write very well; lack of thumbs handicaps them I guess. We did not meet the demands, and the penguin was found dead. How can you ascertain how a hard foam penguin is really dead you might ask? We knew he was dead because there was an arrow through his head. After that, penguins disappeared from the mantle at an alarming rate and began turning up dead in horrible and inventive ways. Threatening notes were left at the scene of the crime as well—something about polar bears and grease. It was funny in a gruesome, horrible way. There was even a double, cross-species murder of a sheep and a penguin and a duck. I can't even tell you how it was done; you would never sleep again.

Everyone jumped right into the fun and began searching for clues. M. R. Sellars even helped us investigate. He had, of course, brought with him rubber gloves, crime scene tape, specimen bags and the like. Which can only show you how weird he really is! Ashleen O'Gaia became the crime scene photographer, and she seemed so normal before the whole thing started. Just goes to show that appearances can be deceiving.

Finally the last three penguins turned up dead, on a plate covered in foil, on the food table. Their little heads were severed from their little bodies, and there was blood everywhere. We summoned Sellars and Ashleen. Murv sealed off the area with crime scene tape, which was not such a good idea because no one could get to the food. As Ashleen was photographing the bodies, Beth leaned over and said, "Wow that blood smells just like ketchup." Without missing a beat and never even looking up from her camera, Ashleen replied, "Oh no, honey, that is just what penguin blood smells like."

The funniest thing about the sad end of the sheep and the penguins was that no one on staff did it, or even knew who did. When we finally did find out whom the perps were (see, been hanging with Murv), it was quite a surprise. Crazy, yes we are.

The sixth year, we chose flamingos. Why? Logical really. We had penguins the year before, and it was unseasonable cool for April. Everyone blamed the penguins. So, flamingos, right? They live in Florida where it is warm. I thought we could sit out at night and have boat drinks with little umbrellas in them and listen to Jimmy Buffett CDs. Let me tell you about the weather that year. It rained buckets. Let me amend that again—it rained bathtubs. It rained almost the entire time. We had a wind that blew through the camp and almost took merchant row with it. My feet became permanently wrinkled, and I had to throw away the tennis shoes I was wearing; they were shot beyond redemption. It was cold and wet and miserable. Finally on Saturday, Dorothy Morrison and about thirty other folks gathered in the kitchen (warm and dry) and did a "Swifting of Energy" spell to make the rain go away. After that it only rained after sunset, just like in Camelot. I decided we would only have warm (and dry) weather animals from that point on. I have learned my lesson!

So the next year, I chose Chihuahuas. They come from a hot dry country. We could eat tacos and drink margaritas; it seemed perfect! It was 38 degrees on Saturday night, and we had snow flurries.

One more thing about the year of the flood. When we emerged from the kitchen after we had done the "no rain" spell, the clouds were blowing away, and the sun was trying to peek out. There in the middle of the ritual field sat a guy playing a didgeridoo. Now in case you did not know, this instrument is used to call rain. I thought that Dorothy was going to have a seizure when she saw him. She was so mad she could not even yell at him. It was as if her throat seized up. It was so funny. We sent a thug to kill him and all was well.

Oh Toto, I think we might be in Kansas! — The year of the flamingos, it rained. But it was more that that, it was a deluge. Water ran through the encampment and became rivers and lakes. Tents slid down the hill on rivers of mud. The most exciting moment of the festival came when an unbelievable wind tore through the camp. Looking back on the destruction, I have to wonder if we caught the tail end of a tornado. The skies opened up and dumped bathtubs full of water on us, and a call came over the radio that the merchants needed help. A bunch of people ran out to merchant row to try and help. My first vision of the merchant tents was of people trying to hang on to their tents. Merchandise was blown all over the ground. I looked to see our merchant manager hanging on to his tents with all his strength. He had two pop-up canopies sitting side by side, and he was standing between the two with a hand on the metal framework of each. I could see the strain of the maneuver in his face. Now let me explain that Billy is not a little guy; he is well over 6"4', and he has some meat on that frame. But, I could see that he was losing the battle with the wind, and I feared that any minute he would go parasailing. As I ran to his aid, I could see that everyone in the field was hanging on to tents with grim expressions on their faces. I grabbed one side of his tent and several others came to help as well. We all stood in the pouring rain with a death grip on a tent pole as the wind slammed us. Man, what a sight we were.

After all the madness was over, the damage was not too bad. Everything in merchant row was wet, we all looked like drowned rats, some of the merchandise had blown away. People began to gather it all up. The potters were the hardest hit of all. They lost much of their stock when a huge, heavy shelf was blown over. The potter himself was under that shelf and miraculously was not hurt. He was stunned that the shelf had gone over since he had built it to be strong and sturdy. It was tragic to see so much of their beautiful pottery in pieces all over the place. I wanted to cry.

Lots of folks came to help us put the merchants back together. Many of those folks bought unbroken pieces of pottery. I saw a lot of folks make a trip to that booth during the rest of the weekend and come away with a purchase. Many of them did not really need a new chalice or the like, but they wanted to help. They wanted the folks that had taken such a hit to come out all right for the weekend and not to go home broke. It was a win-win situation. The buyers got a wonderful piece of art, and the sellers had a pretty good money weekend despite the near tragedy. Money changed hands that day, but it was the love and caring of people that was the real exchange. The true, honest unity and friendship of the people on that site will always be a bright spot in my memory.

**Of Mice and Men** — Our festival is in a state campground. There are cabins with bunks, and the bunks have mattresses. The mattresses stay on the bunks all year round. Sometimes PUF is early enough in the season, that we are the first people on site. That is why we go out early to get the place ready. But sometimes we miss things.

One year, we needed to move some mattresses from one cabin to another. That sounds simple and it should have been. Jim, our VIP Wrangler, loaded a mattress in the trunk of his car to move it to the other side of the camp. The mattress was too long to fit in the trunk, and so he left it open.

All of a sudden, screaming came across my radio followed by something unintelligible about a mouse. I was at the main gate and could see Jim's car. He was standing next to it jumping up and down, and there was indeed a tiny mouse that was also in a panic running the length of his car. The poor little thing ran from the trunk to the hood and back again several times. All this while Jim was yelling. I said into the radio (not an easy task because I was about to have a seizure from laughing), "Jim, for godsakes, quick close the trunk!" Just as I said the word "trunk," the little mouse jumped into the trunk and did not come out.

By now, many members of staff were converging on the scene to see who was being murdered. It took me a minute or so to get there because I was still having laughing fits. Jim was still yelling about the mouse, the mouse was too scared to come out, and we had attracted a group of kids to the action. It was decided that the mattress had to come out of the car, so we could get to the mouse. Once that was done, there was no sign of the mouse. He was hiding, and really, I can't say as I blame him. Someone had the bright idea of luring him out with food. Beth brought a banana. What can I say, she is a vegan. I said, "What self-respecting mouse is going to come out of hiding for a banana. Was there no cheese on this site?" But much to my surprise, he took the bait. It had been a long cold winter.

In short order, the mouse got captured, shown off to all the children who thought he was cute, and we got Jim calmed down. The mouse was escorted to the woods and released. And that should have been that.

But no, there is more. That night in the VIP cabin, everyone was giving Jim grief about being afraid of a little tiny mouse. He tried to defend himself, but really there was no defense. Murv had to tell Jim that the mouse would probably come back since he had been fed. That was a bad idea. Jim freaked out some more. But it was prophecy—he did come back. Just as everyone was getting ready for bed, a little mouse ran across the floor heading for Jim's room. Jim placed himself between his room and the mouse and with his foot, tried to guide the mouse toward Murv's room. In doing so, he severely injured the mouse. Murv had to euthanize him. (The mouse, not Jim.) Then drinking had to happen to say farewell to the mouse. It was very sad. Jim felt so guilty.

We did not want to waste his guilt. The next morning when he went to his car, someone had wrapped a band-aid around his Mickey Mouse antenna topper. He still has not forgiven us for that.

I even have a post-PUF animal story. The year of the sheep, all of our PUF VIPs were "sheeped." That is not quite as horrible as it sounds. It means that many people found stuffed sheep on their doorsteps sometime during the festival. Most of the sheep were alone and looking kind of sad. But some of them were in compromising positions and looked kinda confused. Anyway, I got this email from Grey Cat a few weeks after the sheeping.

Hi, gang,

You probably remember that I found a lost (stuffed) sheep on my doorstep last year. Well, my daughter was hired to paint murals in the halls of a nursing home and she got acquainted with one lady who had no personal possessions in her room, nobody ever came to see her and so on. She told me about it and, seeing the sheep right in front of me as she talked, I asked if the lady would like it. My daughter took it to her and she LOVED it and had some sort of story why a sheep was perfect. So my sheep won't be coming back to PUF this year but I feel that it is where it needs to be.

Blessings,
Grey Cat

⋙Guests⋘
Pack a bag. We are going to the festival!

This chapter is for the folks who go to festivals. First I would like to say thanks for coming. You are the reason why we work our fingers to the bone; we want you to have fun, learn something and go home happy. But you have a responsibility too. You have to take part in making the festivals that you go to better and make your experience the best that it can be.

So how do you find a festival to attend? Well, you have to do your homework before you ever pack a bag. Witchvox is the best place to go looking for festivals to attend. There will be a list of festivals in your area or at least close enough so you can drive. Pick out one or two that snag your interest and research them. If they have a website, go there and see what they offer. If there is not enough information to make you happy, contact them directly and get the scoop. Find others that have attended the festival in question and get their opinions if possible. If the festival is a first-year event, this will be impossible, and sometimes you just have to take your chances. Hopefully, there will be a Q&A somewhere that will answer your burning questions, or the organizers will send out a list if you request it. If there is not such an animal, here are the questions you need to ask, and remember the only stupid question is the one not asked. Wow, that sounded very Zen-like.

How much money? Is that price for the length of the festival? Is there a daily breakdown? If you are bringing kids, how much for them? I have been yelled at before and probably will be again about how much we charge for PUF. In my defense I just want to say, it costs money to put on a festival. The bigger the festival and the more BNPs, the more it drives up the costs. Nothing is cheap these days, folks. Most of the people who throw festivals are not engaged in price gouging, they are just trying to break even. Look for festivals in advance so that you have time to save up the money to attend—just like a vacation.

Do be careful of festivals that offer you the moon and stars for a buck-oh-nine. You may find yourself sleeping in trees and scrounging with the squirrels for nuts. In the last few years, many folks have decided that anyone can pull off a festival, and so they underestimate their costs and short-change their guests. That is why you do the research to find out what you are in for at the festival.

What time does the gate open? Can you get in before the official opening time? What time do you have to be off site? What happens if you can't do it? Someone always wants to come early and we say "NO." Here is why; we are not ready for the public until a set time, which is why there is a set time. We go in a day early to get the place cleaned up, run off any critters that have taken up residence in the cabins, and make sure all the drains are working properly. It is impossible to get all this done if there are early birds in the way. As for the people who just won't leave on time, we press-gang them into work. We don't usually have much trouble in that regard.

What if something prevents you from making it to the festival, and you have already paid? What is the refund policy? Is there a refund policy? Get your details on this in case you don't make the festival and want your money back. If you know in advance what the rules are about this, you won't create a situation with the coordinators.

Are there any cabins? Is it tenting only? Do they care if you sleep in your van? Is there a price difference for different accommodations? If there are cabins, are they really sturdy, or do you need to bring a tarp to throw over the roof in case of rain? Do the cabins have doors and windows? (Quit laughing—that is a legitimate question.)

If you intend to bring an RV, you had better ask if the site could accommodate that vehicle. An RV needs a level spot of ground on which to park (or at least somewhat level). If your RV needs electrical hook-ups, are those provided by the site? Is that an extra fee?

Are there bath facilities or do you have to wash in the lake? Good question to ask especially if it is going to be cold. Remember that running water may mean the creek or the river that flows beside the campsite.

If the festival claims the site to be primitive, what does that really mean? We call our site primitive, but it has cabins, a kitchen, running water, bathhouses and electricity. By primitive we mean: don't bring your computer and try to run it in one of the cabins, you will blow fuses; there is only one phone on site, and it usually does not work; there is no glass in most of the windows of the cabins, but there are screens. Compared to some of the sites I have seen, we are not primitive at all, but I don't want anyone to think they will be staying at the Holiday Inn.

Will there be food provided as a part of the entry fee cost? If provided, how many meals will be included? Will the food be extra? Will there be food vendors? Do you have to bring your own food? What do the festival planners consider to be a meal? A bologna sandwich, bag of chips and an RC cola do not make a meal in my world. Get the food facts.

Will there be activities for the kids? What responsibility do the parents have for the planned activities? Do you have to handcuff your kid to your leg for the weekend?

Will you have to work community service time? How much time do you have to donate? Most festivals require it; we could not pull off PUF without the help of our guests.

Are the classes extra? Do any of the workshops have a fee for materials? Some do and some don't, you have to ask.

Ask everything you can think of, and there will be no surprises when you get to the festival. It will make your stay much more enjoyable.

I have a list of things that the festival promoters may not tell you. Leave your bad attitude at home. A festival is supposed to be fun. If you hit the gate in a bad mood, you will spread that around. No one needs that. You will find yourself wondering why everyone at the festival seems to be avoiding you.

Leave your Witch Wars at home. This kind of nonsense has no place at a festival. Actually, it has no place at all. Disengage from whatever grudges you may hold, and try to be spiritually minded—or at least polite. Of course, you may run into people who have given you a hard time in the past, or even in the last week. But you can be the bigger person. Don't wander around the site bad-mouthing the other person or people. Keep your opinions to yourself. Don't try to get people to be on your side. A festival is neutral ground, like Switzerland without the snow or the money or the chocolate…nevermind. A festival site is usually a big place; you should be able to avoid someone you don't like. It is certainly not the place to call someone out publicly and air your grievances.

Try to keep your domestic problems private. No one wants to hear the argument you are having with your significant other. Of course, it will give everyone something juicy to gossip about for weeks after the festival has ended. (Maybe years depending on the entertainment value of the argument.)

If the event is not a clothing-optional event, for the love-o-gods, keep your clothes on! Try to understand that if the festival is not clothing optional, there is probably a good reason for it. In many states, nudity in front of minors is considered child sexual abuse. In my state of mind, depending on who is naked, it can be adult sexual abuse. It is a fact of life that the very people who you don't want to see naked are usually the first ones to get naked.

While we are on the subject of naked; please read all of the information associated with the festival that you intend to attend. You do not want to get to a festival, pay your money, set up your camp, look around you and notice that many of the people are wearing nothing but pentacles. Especially if you are too modest to do the same. Conversely, don't get all wrapped around the axle if you get to a festival, walk out of your tent wearing nothing but a pentangle and carrying a cup of coffee only to find that everyone is clothed and staring at you. If you do not get all the information on the festival before you hit site, then you have no one to blame but yourself. Do not expect the festival organizers to change the rules for you. Do your homework.

If you are taking children, find out if there are activities for them and sign them up. This will give you a great opportunity to see what a day is like without having someone attached to your ankle. But please remember that they are your children, and no one owes you the watching of them. Pay attention to them, where they are, what they are doing and whom they are doing it with while at festival. Most of us do have a tendency to watch out for other people's children, but that does not relieve you of the responsibility.

You are the main ingredient in a festival. Without you, there is no point. I want you to embrace the experience and find new friends, learn new things, commune with the gods and grow. That is what it is all about. Bless you and Happy Trails.

❧Last But Not Least❦
Twenty-five rules for a festival organizer

Well, this will be a few more than that. First let's talk about money for a moment. You have to figure out how to price your festival fees so that you don't bankrupt yourself.

- ❏ Site. This is one of the biggest costs to deal with. You must shop for something that is reasonable, and you must start looking for a site long in advance of your festival. The good places go fast. We reserve our site one year in advance.
- ❏ Food for the weekend. You really want to keep this cost under $6 per person, and yes, that is possible. If you compare prices, watch the sales and plan ahead, you can manage this.
- ❏ All of the extras: paper towels, toilet paper, cleaner, light bulbs, batteries, etc. Make this list now. Really think about everything that you have planned for the festival and add the items you need. Include oven mitts; we always forget those.
- ❏ Advertising. You may have to pay someone to create graphics and flyers for you. If you hand-deliver them to shops in your area, include the cost of gas.
- ❏ Printing. This will cost more than you realize. You must have the flyers printed—and the programs. In short, anything that you will be handing out at festival or before festival.
- ❏ Mailing costs. If you intend to send information out to shops within a certain radius of your festival, mailing is the best way to go. Include the price of mailing tubes or large envelopes in your cost.
- ❏ Insurance. This is a big expense for a festival. You need to call every insurance company in the book. Ask if they underwrite a venture such as yours. Explain that the activities for the weekend will include workshops and meals. Tell them that it is a calm weekend; they will get a little nervous if you tell them that you will have firewalkers and a rock-and-roll band. They will want to know your head count; this is something you can estimate. Try and find an insurance broker that will price the coverage with many different carriers; that way you will get the best price. Prepare for sticker shock. Why do you need

insurance? In a perfect world, Pagans would not sue other Pagans. But alas, this is not a perfect world, and you want to make sure you are covered. Besides, if someone broke a leg at your festival and had no insurance, wouldn't you be glad that you could cover that? Of course you would. You may be able to forgo this expense in the first couple of years of your festival while the numbers are small and you know most of the people attending. But once you go beyond family, you had better insure yourself.

- Incorporation. Ah, to incorporate or not to incorporate, that is the question. There are good reasons to do it. The corporation is liable, not you personally; no one can take your house, your vehicles or your dogs in a dispute. Plus, it seems that insurance companies and the like are much more comfortable dealing with XYZ, Inc. than plain ole Joe Shmoe.
- Website. If you intend to grow, you will need one. The costs include someone to design it (unless you have a friend with that talent), a place to put it and a domain name.
- Ice. You will need this if you are going to keep food cold without the benefit of refrigeration. But you will also need it to ice down drinks at meals. We have had it delivered in 40 pound bags and trucked it in ourselves. After we totaled up all the ice receipts, we found that the delivery was a lot cheaper and much easier.
- Port-a-johns. If there are no bathrooms on your site, this is something that you will need. The cost is not too terrible, and they will deliver and pick-up.
- Gifts for VIPs. This is something that we do to show our appreciation to our special guests. Every year it varies depending on what kinds of crazy things we find. It usually includes a basket with chocolate, coffee, snacks, and sometimes socks, underwear and coffee mugs emblazoned with our mascot of the year.
- Fees for VIPs. This can run from a little gas money up to a hefty speaking fee. Some speakers will show up for a meal, a bed and a place to sell their books and maybe read tarot as well. When you first start out, these folks are a boon to your pocket.
- Transportation for VIPs. This can be $50 for gas or a plane ticket from an exotic port.

- **Miscellaneous.** This is the category that you throw everything else into; it gives you a pad for the things you forgot to include in your original figures. It doesn't have to be much; allow 100 bucks for this.

Add up all the costs, and try not to freak out. This will give you the amount you will spend overall. This is where the fun comes into the picture. You now have to decide how much you will charge your guests. You don't want to go too low or you might get in hot water, too high and you might price yourself out of the market. Remember, you are selling a commodity, and it has to be worth the price. Also, remember that while this is a labor of love, it is also business and you must at the very least break even.

Let's say that your expenses are $2000.00. After much thought, you decide that you would like to charge $35 for the weekend for an adult. Ok, divide $2000 by 35 and that will give you the break-even number of people that need to attend. It is 55, so make that number 56 and that gives you a few dollars over $2000.00. More than that and you are golden; less than that, you are in the hole. Be sure that you count only the number of paying adults, not children or your staff.

I wish you much good luck and many blessings on your endeavor. Here are a few rules for you to follow:

1. Don't take yourself too seriously; this is not brain surgery. If you don't have fun with it, no one else is going to either.
2. Find yourself some good, reliable people for staff members.
3. Delegate. If you do not understand what that word means, look it up.
4. Keep a tight grip on the purse strings.
5. Get a good pair of walking shoes.
6. Pack sunscreen.
7. Sleep at every opportunity that you find.
8. Smile, this ain't gonna kill you.
9. Plan everything, plan everything, plan everything.
10. Write everything down.

Last But Not Least

11. Practice saying "NO." Do it in front of a mirror till you get it right.
12. Stop and eat something during festival, or you will fall down.
13. Don't let anyone talk you into something that you think is a bad idea.
14. Don't let anyone talk you out of something that you think is a good idea.
15. Make a list of everyone that you deal with, buy from, etc. Keep it for next year. That will save you the legwork of finding those folks again.
16. Compare prices.
17. Don't let anyone push your buttons. Remain calm under fire.
18. Pack extra socks.
19. Get a hat. You will be running around in the sun a lot.
20. Bring lots of change. You can't have enough $1s, $5s or quarters.
21. Get a cell phone.
22. Remember this is a labor of love.
23. Price your tickets so that you will not go into the hole.
24. Don't get drunk until the last night of festival.
25. You cannot do it all and be it all the first year, or even the second. Start small and you will survive to do it again next year.

Ok, that's it. It is all the knowledge, warning and information I have to impart after ten years of running a festival. I hope you find it helpful. I hope that you are as lucky as I have been to find the best people to help you in your quest, to have as much fun as I have had, to make the wonderful friends that I have made along this journey. It has been and remains a wonderful experience. Would I do it all over again? You betcha.

Index

Adult waiver, 137
Advertising, 33-36, 56, 104, 110, 168
Alcohol, 15, 39, 47, 65, 141
Allergic, Allergies, 27, 41, 138-139, 151
Anglo-Saxon, 10
Antibacterial, 78
Asatru, 9, 10
Athame, 1, 131
Big-Nose Pagan (BNP), Big-Nose Witch, 5-7, 13, 15, 20, 52, 54, 63, 70, 123-127, 164
Bonewits, Isaac, 10, 52, 63, 125
Budget, 20, 23, 68, 82, 91, 125, 126
Buddhist, 54
Bug spray, 74, 78
Camping, 19, 21, 26, 30, 32, 35, 37, 39, 44, 56, 59, 75, 80, 139, 141
Candles, 43, 45, 64, 65, 75, 78, 128, 132, 149
Cell phone, 59, 65, 171
Central meeting point, 7-9
Child, Children, 1, 4, 5, 9, 21, 26, 27, 33, 41-47, 61, 67, 70-73, 105, 128, 129, 134, 135, 138-139, 143, 145-147, 151, 162, 167, 170
Clothing optional (see also **Nudity**), 11, 31, 33, 144, 167
Community service (see also **Volunteer**), 26, 134, 136, 141, 166
Contract, 55, 126, 140-142
Coordinator, 19, 21, 46, 53, 140, 141
Coven, 1, 8, 10, 13, 14, 15, 34, 49, 62, 68
Daytrip, 37
Drugs, 4, 65, 70, 80, 144, 151
Druid, 7, 8, 10, 156
Duct tape, 74, 77
Drinking, Drunk, 4, 5, 39, 65, 69, 145, 162, 171
Drummer, Drumming, Drum, 8, 9, 44, 47, 66, 70, 80, 105, 145, 147
EMT, 69, 151, 155

Etiquette, 15, 51, 64, 146
Feast, 62, 66, 79, 84, 90, 136
Fees, 30, 31, 40, 124, 126, 139, 143, 149, 165, 166, 169
Festival coordinator, 19
Fire pit, 30, 32, 67, 145, 148, 149
Flyers, 6, 23, 33-36, 39, 58, 59, 168
Food, 10, 15, 16, 20, 23, 25, 29, 31, 32, 33, 35, 36, 37, 40, 60-62, 66, 67, 70, 79, 82-91, 107, 124, 126, 129, 134-135, 146, 156, 162, 166, 168, 169
General Pagan Festival, 6
Gifts, 169
Grey Cat, 15, 51, 52, 123, 162-163
Group discount, 39, 40
Guedra, 9, 47
Heathen, 8, 10
Hindu, 54
Ice, 29, 79, 90-91, 93, 102, 103, 152, 169
ID bracelets, 27, 71, 75, 145
Inappropriate, 73, 145
Incorporation, 169
Indoor festival, 29
Insurance, 137, 138, 140, 168-169
Kail, Tony, 16, 50, 51, 52, 123
Kitchen, 9, 20, 30, 32, 70, 71, 75, 82-83, 84, 86-90, 102, 103, 134, 135, 136, 145, 147, 165
Kitchen Witch, 20, 82, 85, 86
Lost & Found, 75
Map, 6, 38, 58-59, 110
Merchant (see also **Vendor**), 7, 9, 17, 21, 26, 35, 55-59, 66, 76, 84, 91, 105, 106, 110, 135, 139-143, 151, 159, 160
Merchant Manager/coordinator, 21, 140-141, 160
Minor, 11, 73, 167
Minor waiver, 138
Morrison, Dorothy, 52, 83, 159
Nudity (see also **Clothing Optional**), 144, 167
O'Gaia, Ashleen, 52, 158-159

Index

Pagan Pride day, 13
Pain-in-the-ass, 37
Paramedic, 155
PayPal, 35, 38-39
Pedophile, 72-73
Permit, 104, 105, 106, 129, 130
Pets, 146
Port-a-john, port-a-potty, 30, 57, 169
Pre-registration, 25, 37-40, 44, 83
Prices, 68, 88, 110, 125, 135, 168, 171
Printing, 110, 168
Radical Fairies, 10
Recipes, 82, 92-103
Refund, 40, 66, 140, 146, 165
Ritual, 1, 5, 6, 8, 10, 14, 15, 21, 25, 31, 32, 35, 49, 51, 57, 60-65, 66, 83, 107, 110, 131, 152, 153, 159
Security, 20, 141
Security Thugs, 20, 46, 154
Sellars, M. R. (Murv), 36, 51, 52, 53, 123, 158-159, 162
Sign, 11, 21, 58-59, 76, 125
Site, 9, 11, 29-32, 35, 37, 38, 42, 51, 58, 59, 62, 68, 71, 86, 90, 104, 106, 110, 129, 134, 135, 145, 149, 165-166, 168,
Society of Creative Anachronisms, 15
Sunscreen, 1, 76, 80, 170
Tape, 74, 77
Teen, 21, 44, 47, 71, 85, 135, 145
Teen Tuner, 21
Telesco, Trish, 52
Tent camping, 25, 26, 30, 31, 32, 37, 39, 47, 56, 59, 70, 80, 165
Things to bring as a coordinator, 74-77
Things to bring if you are coming to play, 78-81
Transportation, 169
Vendor (see also **Merchant**), 25, 55, 57, 91, 105, 142, 166
VIP (see also **Big-Nose Pagan**), 7, 21, 23, 35, 37, 84, 162, 169
VIP Wrangler, 20, 161

Volunteer(see also **Community Service**), 18, 26, 42, 43, 44, 46, 49, 62, 86, 134-136, 145, 148, 151
Waiver, 32, 35, 68, 77, 137, 138
Website, 20, 34-35, 38-40, 45, 51, 58, 59, 123, 124, 125, 164, 169
Wiccans, 7-8, 60, 130
Witchvox, 34, 164
Wodening, Swain, 52
Workshop, 5, 6, 8, 9, 10, 13, 15, 16, 17, 20, 25, 35, 41, 43, 45, 49-54, 70, 76, 83, 104, 105, 110, 123, 124, 126, 132, 166, 168
Workshop Guru/Coordinator, 20, 53
Yoga, 54

Tish Owen is a woman of abundance. She is a daughter, a mother, a grandmother, a wife, a friend, a shop owner, an author, a seamstress, a sailor, a brewer. She reads tarot cards professionally and is the coordinator of the Pagan Unity Festival. Ten years ago she started with what she thought was a good idea, and that has now grown into the largest Pagan festival in the mid-South. Through the trials and tribulations of facilitating it each year, she has garnered a wealth of knowledge which she wants to share with others so that no one has to reinvent the wheel.

She currently resides in Nashville, Tennessee with her husband Patrick, and a cast of characters starting with a very silly Rottweiler, a cat who bosses everybody, an Amazon Grey parrot who knows too much for her own good and a Vietnamese Fire-bellied tree frog. She loves her life and is grateful for more things than there is room to list here.

www.ingramcontent.com/pod-product-compliance
Lightning Source LLC
Chambersburg PA
CBHW070735020526

44118CB00035B/1366